Authentic Brand Academy™

Table of Contents

Insight   1

STRATEGIC PLANNING

1. In Pursuit of Authenticity   3
  What a Brand Image is Not   5
  Perception & the Brand Image   6
  Touchpoints; Forging Connections   7
  Dollars & Sense (Or, Why Brand Matters)   10
**2. Authentic Brands are Whole-Brain Brands: Brand Maestros
  are Whole Brain Thinkers**   13
  How the human brain works   13
  Authentic branding requires whole-brain thinking   18
  Authentic brands are holistic brands   20
  Which kind of smarts do you have?   21
  How we make decisions: Emotion, intuition and brand strategy   27
3. From Napkin Idea to Authentic Master Strategy — Part I   34
  The modern brand: Building to compete   35
    20th Century Brand Strategy   36
    21st Century Brand Strategy   36
  Authenticity starts with your brand's philosophy, values & vision   38
  Brand architecture: Building the house   42
  What is your message   46

Making the promise   48

Who is your target?   50

4. From Napkin Idea to Authentic Master Strategy — Part II:
Differentiation   **55**

Whatever happened to the USP   55

Are you different? You'd better be.   60

Lay of the land: your position in the brandscape   61

Differentiation tactics   63

5. From Napkin Idea to Authentic Master Strategy — Part III:
Personality   **76**

What is brand personality?   76

Brand characters   80

Beware the Sybil Effect   81

Language and pictures have personality, too   83

6. The Brand Experience   **94**

Touchpoints are the experience   95

Branding for the senses   98

Building a persuasive brand   102

7. Telling an Authentic Story   **107**

EXECUTION

8. The Design Revolution (Innovating and Differentiating through
Authentic Brand Design)   **113**

How important is design?   114

The feminizing of design   117

Visual assets are financial assets   118

The package it comes in   131

Intuitive web design   133

9. Authentic Execution & The Business of Brand   **137**

Extending the brand identity across all touchpoints   137

Planning the execution   139

The complete brand campaign: Integrating your touchpoints   142

Internal branding: Internal touchpoints count, too   148

Shortening the sell-through trajectory 150
Maximizing your Brand Ecosystem 152
    Expand your brand market space 152
    Expand your core customer base 152
    What are your sales goals? 154

MANAGEMENT

10. Managing the Brand for Equity & Value 156
Auditing your brand 156
Stick to the rules: Brand Guidelines 158
Dazzle your stakeholders: Presentations to investors and buyers 159
Predicting the future: It's about the category 160
    The secret to winning brand battles 161
    Competition is a good thing 163
When to kill the brand, and when to reinvent 164
Brand crisis management: Combating negative publicity 166
Go forth and be authentic 168

Insight

What you are about to read may change the way you view branding forever. When you finish this book, you will be equipped to build an authentic brand from scratch — step by step, inch by inch.

Over the years, my company, HOW Creative, has been privileged to work with some extraordinary clients whose brands have left a distinctive mark on the world — Disney, Xerox, Apple, Philips, DreamWorks, ABC Networks, Mattel, Fox, Honda and Fujitsu — to name a few. These rich and diverse experiences have allowed me to develop and refine a complete branding process — from the napkin idea to the product in the customer's hands, from strategy to execution to managing the brand. This process has crafted compelling brands that were welcomed into big-box retail spaces such as Nordstrom's, Macy's, Toys R Us, Costco, Walgreen's, Target and Wal-Mart. This process has added to our client's bottom lines, and to the equity and value of their brands.

This process — the process you will learn in this valuable book — works for any business, any service, any product. It works for both B2B and B2C brands, from start-ups to Fortune 100 companies. It works in every industry, every brand category and every market segment.

This process will turbo boost a brand's awareness and resonance in the marketplace — shaving off years of frustration and unfulfilled marketing dreams, preventing millions of dollars worth of mistakes. You will learn how to build profits, value and equity in a few short years, not decades — even months, for some brands. You will learn how to create new brand opportunities and categories and mold a brand into an industry leader.

To succeed in the new economy, a brand must connect with the customer's heart, gut, and mind. Modern brand-building is both an art and a science; a process that fuses creative spark with technical know-how, each in the right proportion.

My passion is helping organizations transform products and services into rich brand experiences that motivate and inspire from the inside out and helping consumers achieve their aspirations. As a professional brand strategist, this is the motto I live by, and my source of inspiration for this book.

If I had to sum up the secret to successful branding in one word, that word would be *"Authenticity"*. Over the years, I have traveled the globe… launching new brands, revitalizing old brands, speaking at brand strategy seminars. I am convinced, that thousand of conversatins later, long term success in the marketplace comes to brand authenticity. Much has been written about brand-building, but rarely does anyone discuss the process of building *authenticity*.

What is an *authentic brand?* There is a short answer and a long answer.

The short answer is this: It is a brand so authentic that it would be difficult (if not impossible) to duplicate. An authentic brand is original, genuine, real, true, authoritative, convincing and trustworthy.

The long answer is the rest of this book.

Markets evolve over time. Brands come and go. But in the long-run, authenticity always wins. And for authentic brands, the potential is limitless. This book will show you how to reach for the stars.

This book will show you how to build, execute and manage an authentic brand.

① In Pursuit of Authenticity

Once upon a time (back in the 20th Century), we tended to favor the mass marketing approach. We threw a lot of mud at the wall, figuring that at least some of it would stick. The mud that stuck we called "market share."

In the new economy, mass marketing will not launch a brand, maintain a brand, or save a brand. Mass marketing is dead. It is not that the *masses* have vanished. They are out there, bigger than ever, and always desperate to find products they can believe in. That is the good news. Problem is, it is harder to get their attention — harder still to sustain it over the life of your brand.

Company's struggle to communicate their messages because jaded consumers refuse to pay attention. Consumers listen to their friends instead of listening to a company's advertising. As a result, most brands remain invisible.

In the old economy, if we tinkered with the product at all, it was, perhaps, to add a couple of new features and benefits. In the new economy, we let the *customer* choose features and benefits; consider the Mini Cooper philosophy, for example. Tailor your Mini Cooper to your own personal tastes. Yes, W.I.I.F.M. (What's In It For Me?) is alive and well.

In the old economy, the communication frequency was "monologue." In the new economy, the communication frequency is "dialogue." Brand is a two-way conversation, between you and the customer. And guess who controls that conversation? The customer holds all the cards. They can tune you out in a nanosecond.

Old marketing tactics have been shattered by the fragmentation of existing media and the emergence of new media. Customers have instant access to massive reservoirs of information, which they can pass along to their friends with the click of a button. And brands live and die by the information that customers choose to pass along.

In this brave new world, organizations that underestimate the influence of word of mouth do so at their own peril. Ideas ripple across the internet at warp speed. An "idea," for example, may simply be a brand. After all, what is a brand if not an idea? In a matter of days — potentially, hours — a few cranky customers can completely redefine your brand.

On the other hand, a few satisfied customers can build an army of new believers without you having to lift a finger.

As Malcolm Gladwell so eloquently points out in his 2004 book, *The Tipping Point:*

> The world around us can seem immovable. It isn't. The slightest push — in just the right place — can tip it.

This is both good news and bad news for the branding strategist, since the customer, whose behavior you are attempting to motivate, is so easily influenced by external forces.

In the new economy, getting noticed — and starting a dialogue — is further complicated by the choice explosion. Consumers have more product choices than ever — in practically every market niche — and less and less time to sift them, or perhaps we have simply become too impatient to sift them. This is not a passing fad. It is the new market reality.

Truth is, products often seem equal to us in terms of features and benefits, so we look for shortcuts to help us make quick buying decisions. Trust, more often than not, is that shortcut. As a result, trust emerges from the customer perception of authenticity.

In the new economy, *brand authenticity* has become more than just another buzz phrase for brand strategists to toss around to impress clients. It has become an essential business asset.

Let us begin the quest for authenticity by dispelling some common myths…

What a Brand Image is *not:*

- A logo
- A corporate identity
- Marketing, advertising or graphic design
- A company, a product or service
- A name on a label

An authentic brand is much bigger than any of its attributes.

A brand is a feeling and an emotional reaction. It is an experience. Brand authenticity, is judged by the heart, the gut, and the mind. Humans are intuitive, emotional beings, and they do not invest in a brand until they *feel something* for the brand. A brand encompasses the customer's overall experience.

Without the emotional connection, a logo is just a logo. No corporate identity package can forge an emotional bond; it has no way to engage the consumer, no touchpoints from which to forge connections. It just announces: "Here we are," not "Here's *who* we are."

Your brand is a promise, plus your delivery on that promise…time and time again. Delivering on your brand promise is how you build trust. Trust is that intangible, intuitive silent partner that we rely on to help us make buying decisions. In the absence of a more compelling reason, we will buy what we trust.

Brands are defined by the customer's personal expectation and their experiences with the company, product or service. The customer experience is about *value.* It is what they got in exchange for their money and their trust. If you are late shipping, don not reply to emails, or sell products that don not deliver what you promised, your brand is on its way to extinction. The interactive nature of today's media allows customers to share their experiences. And share they will — count on it.

Branding has become more about what you actually *do* than what you *say* you will do.

PERCEPTION AND THE BRAND IMAGE

Why do people choose one product over another? More often than not, the reason is brand. Brand is the reason one company dominates its competitors. Market share is usually a testament to the power of the brand in the customer's mind, not necessarily the product's superior quality. Yes, it is true: It is quite possible to create a high-quality brand without having a high-quality product.

In fact, brand is such powerful stuff that a company can initially succeed simply by being a brand name. But ultimately, if your product or service isn't up to snuff, it will come back to bite you. Dissatisfied customers will make you pay. And your brand could die a quick — and possibly mortifyingly public — death.

Delighted customers, on the other hand, will rave about you to a few hundred thousand of their closest friends. Meet and beat your customer's expectations the first time, the second time, every time, and you will forge an emotional bond that can lasts a brand lifetime.

Consider the Red Cross brand. During 2005's Hurricane Katrina in New Orleans, Louisiana, the Red Cross was ubiquitous, mobilizing resources in the eye of the storm and in the glare of the media spotlight — shaming other incompetent government agencies who never seemed to do anything fast enough and that was not just a one-time thing. The Red Cross delivers on an ongoing basis. Whenever there is a disaster, the Red Cross reaches out to devastated victims, inviting them to come forward for help, to register with the web site SafeAndWell.org (a domain name that sends a powerful brand message in itself), or to call a toll-free number if they can not access the Internet. SafeAndWell.org publishes information about victims so that friends and family from outside the disaster area can get updates on their loved ones.

What matters most is who customers think you are, their perception of your brand — that is your *brand image.* Your *brand identity* is the thing you intended to build, the perception you meant to create, the impression you meant to imprint in the customer's mind.

Brand values are what your brand stands for, the core set of values that sum up your brand. *We are a premium quality brand. A prestige brand. A value brand. A disposable brand. An innovative brand. We are about fun in the sun. Exercise and energy. Environmental responsibility.*

Inauthentic brands emerge when there's a disconnect between a company's brand values, brand identity and brand image. In authentic brands, brand values, brand identity and brand image are perfectly aligned.

If you manufacture a car that you tout as the most fuel-efficient car in its class, but according to all the consumer product reviews and customer opinion surveys, the little sucker is actually a gas-guzzler that offers the worst gas mileage on the road, there is a disconnect between the brand identity you have crafted and the brand's image and true values. You have got an inauthentic brand.

The bottom line? Brand is not who you say *you* are. It is who the customer says you are.

How does *the customer* decide who you are? They decide through encounters with your touchpoints.

TOUCHPOINTS: FORGING CONNECTIONS

The shortest distance between your brand message and your targeted customer is a touchpoint.

What is a touchpoint? Every tangible and intangible contact point between the customer and your product or service. A touchpoint is a medium, anything and everything that communicates and expresses the value of your brand to a customer — from a customer's first glimpse of your product to a phone conversation with your customer service department; from a media interview with your CEO to your product packaging.

The second your product or service reaches a prospect, you have made an impression. That is your first touchpoint. That touchpoint might be a glimpse of your brand icon (referred to by many as a logo) on a product package or a casual mention of your product or service by a customer to a friend.

A customer experiences a service or product by hearing the brand name, seeing an ad, seeing the product, or actually using the service or product. Each experience shapes an idea or *impression* of the brand. When you hear the word *Amazon,* do you instantly think of the second largest river in the world? Or do you think of those little brown cardboard boxes showing up on your doorstep?

Impressions can be images and associations… photographic snapshots, colors, a brand icon, memories, words. The impression evolves with each subsequent re-experiencing of the brand — each additional touchpoint. Customer opinions about a product are driven by their experiences with the product, their chemistry with the product, their feelings and impulses — both conscious and unconscious.

Every brand impression counts. Every voice mail, every greeter in your store, every glimpse of your company or product name, colors, layout, logo, brand icon, tagline — they are all touchpoints.

A brand's touchpoints must be strategically integrated — designed to communicate the overall experience of your brand identity. All your touchpoints should be designed to support your brand promise, which reflects your core values and corporate culture. The cumulative effect can be powerful. You want your brand to be a billboard in the consumer's mind, a freeze-frame — not a fleeting thought.

Touchpoints connect a company's brand identity to its brand image. Touchpoints are the first step toward creating brand equity. Effectively, they are a set of assets linked to the brand's name and symbol that enhance the value of the product or service.

The primary asset categories are:

> **Brand name awareness** — brand presence in the consumer's mind — the billboard
>
> **Brand loyalty,** achieved through loyalty-building programs
>
> **Perceived quality,** which is usually at the heart of what customers are buying
>
> **Brand associations** — emotional, self-expressions, benefits, functional benefits

How will you stand out from the pack? Authentic touchpoints can differentiate you from all other competitors and establish clarity and direction for all of your stakeholders. Touchpoints can define a brand experience so singular that your brand becomes a billboard, and your competitors become fleeting thoughts. Authentic brands can penetrate, and even dominate, ostensibly saturated markets.

Without a strong brand, you have no identity. No story. No promise. You stand for nothing in the marketplace. Living brands are ultimately either respected or disrespected, trusted or not trusted. The disrespected and untrusted will eventually die. Many of the rest are invisible.

But a powerful, authentic brand has a distinctive brand personality that customers can connect to emotionally. Touchpoints help mold that personality. People often choose brands that stand for ideas and aspirations that they themselves possess, or want to possess. We actually perceive brands as having personality traits. In fact, people often choose their brands the same way they choose their friends. In addition to skills, talents, personality traits, and physical characteristics, they simply like them as people.

Think of brand personality as the unique set of human personality traits that are applicable to and relevant for a brand. Personality is an individual's way of *being* in the world. Personality usually has nothing to do with the cognitive aspects of a person's behavior (e.g., intelligence, ability, knowledge). Personality always revolves around the emotional and dynamic aspects. Personality is experienced and evaluated by others on an emotional level.

Human personality is composed of traits or markers that are (as Freud would tell you) dynamic and cumulative, but, above all, durable and relatively stable over time. That holds true with brands, brand personality must be a constellation of stable, persistent traits. Since brands are often personified by consumers (perceived as people), human personality descriptors (adjectives) can be used to describe brands.

One thing to always remember about brand personality is that it will shine through whether you intend for it to or not. (As with human personality!) So intend it. Control it. Hone it. Project a unique personality on purpose.

DOLLARS AND SENSE (OR, WHY BRAND MATTERS)

Branding, ultimately, is the most important business language. Your brand's value will be reflected in your company's bottom line. Put another way: Your brand will either be an asset or a liability.

Does a brand have a dollar value? Absolutely. Look at Coca Cola, ranked by Interbrand as the number one global brand in 2008. Coca Cola has a brand value of $66.7 billion, but thanks to the brand's equity, Coca Cola's market cap, including brand value, is in the neighborhood of $110 billion. Clearly the Coca Cola brand is an enormous financial asset to Coca Cola, the company — arguably, its single greatest financial asset.

On the other hand, once a brand becomes a liability, it has no value, no market and no future. If you don not believe it, consider the Ford Pinto, whose tendency to catch fire ultimately incinerated its value in the marketplace, to say nothing of the impact on Ford's bottom line. It no longer mattered that the Pinto had an "affordable" price tag; the risk of hazard made it unaffordable. Ford, wisely, stopped building the Pinto.

Take a look at some of the ways brand assets become financial assets...

- An authentic brand is the most efficient path to overcoming consumers objections and closing sales. A powerful brand, in fact, *pre-sells*. Cleverly branded products sell themselves. Products with colorless, indistinctive brand identities must rely on constant promotions to thrive — or for that matter, even survive.

- Authenticity is a secret propelling force: An authentic brand boosts marketing momentum through word of mouth (a.k.a., *buzz*), which, in the new economy, can make or break a brand. If everyone is talking about you, you do not have to spend as much money to promote yourself.

- An authentic brand should be an asset, aesthetically, for aesthetic assets impact financial assets. Aesthetics matter — from the brand icon/logo to product design and product packaging. Distinctive, strategic design can propel a brand to exciting new heights. Aesthetics can be so powerful that they come to define a brand. Consider the design aesthetic of the Aston Martin, conforming to Aston Martin's brand message of the "fine, civilized high performance sports car." No other sports car quite looks like an Aston Martin, does it? No doubt Aston Martin aficionados would tell you that no other car quite drives like it, either.

  Aesthetics (especially when coupled with innovative functional design) can even build a brand leader and define an entire market or category, relegating all imitators to the leftover scraps of market share. Microsoft's me-too player Zune has infiltrated only a fraction of the media player market, compared to Apple's sleek original, the iPod.

  Aesthetics, in fact, are so powerful that they can turn a common commodity product into a premium product; for example, the Mini Cooper or Apple's desktop and laptop computers.

- An authentic brand is the most powerful up-pricing strategy around. Consumers will pay a premium for the brand on the label if they believe the brand to be premium.

- An authentic brand is a strategic partner magnet. Build a powerful brand and other companies will flock to you because they will believe that lending your name to their products helps guarantee their success. Authentic brands attract lots of new friends, and keep the old ones.

- An authentic brand builds affinity…and future sales. Once customers experience the quality of one product sold under your company brand, they will be naturally inclined to buy future products from you, even when faced with keenly competitive products.

- An authentic brand builds customer loyalty. Customer loyalty in today's fickle marketplace is rare and valuable. There are, in the end, four classes of consumers: Prospects, customers, loyal customers, and former customers. It is no secret that it is cheaper, faster, and easier to keep an existing customer than it is to attract a new one.

- An authentic brand is equity, should you someday decide to sell your company. Personnel may change, geography may change, markets may change — an authentic brand does not.

- An authentic brand has clear intention that can be measured by clear results: brand value, profits, and equity. In the end, business is always about results.

Convinced yet? Want an authentic brand of your own? Let's get started…

Authentic Brands are Whole-Brain Brands:

Brand Maestros Are Whole-Brain Thinkers

HOW THE HUMAN BRAIN WORKS

Each of us has a left brain and a right brain — or more accurately, a left brain hemisphere and a right brain hemisphere. Each of these two brain hemispheres has its own ideas about you should evaluate information and make decisions, and each has a tendency to battle the other for control of your actions. In other words, you effectively have two minds — two separate spheres of consciousness.

You will need both of them to build an authentic brand, which means you must teach them to get along with each other.

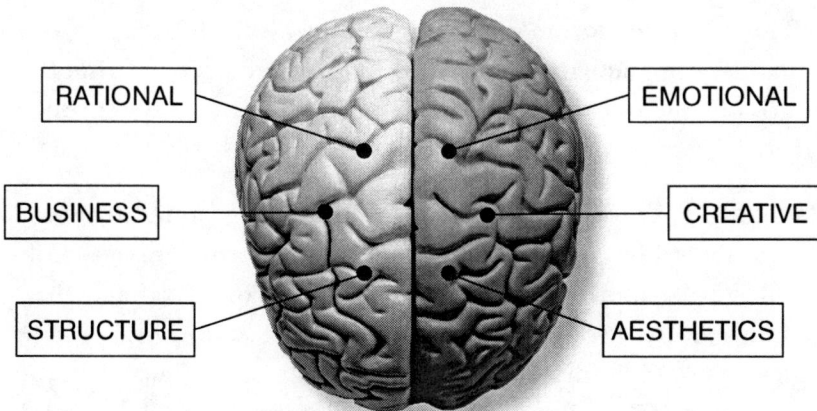

RATIONAL   EMOTIONAL

BUSINESS   CREATIVE

STRUCTURE   AESTHETICS

Anatomically speaking, each hemisphere is a mirror image of the other in that most brain structures are present in both hemispheres. Func-

tionally, however, each hemisphere has its own areas of mental special-
ization, a phenomenon known as "brain lateralization." For example,
the left hemisphere is practical, logical, rational, analytical and
sequential, while the right hemisphere is intuitive, emotional, visual,
and creative.

In the left hemisphere, logic rules; the left hemisphere likes to break
things down into logical patterns, form a strategy, hatch a plan. The left
hemisphere processes information in an analytical and sequential way,
first analyzing the pieces, then putting them together to form a whole
picture. In the right hemisphere, imagination rules; the right hemisphere likes the holistic approach. The right hemisphere, being highly
visuospatial, likes to take in the whole picture first, then synthesize and
process information simultaneously.

The left hemisphere is most commonly deployed for traditional
business functions; the right hemisphere for creative functions.
But we will come back to that in a minute.

When it comes to communication between the left and right hemispheres, the corpus callosum is where most of the action happens. The
corpus callosum is a massive band of nerve tissue, an arched bridge of
nerve tissue whose fibers connect the right and left hemispheres of the
brain. The corpus callosum facilitates communication between — and
coordinates — the activities of the two hemispheres. Otherwise, they
would not be able to communicate with each other and synchronize
data at all.

This fascinating discovery of "brain lateralization" resulted from research conducted by Nobel prize winner and American psychobiolo-
gist, Dr. Roger W Sperry in the 1960s. Sperry discovered that if this
bridge between the two hemispheres, the corpus callosum, is damaged
or surgically severed (for example, to relieve epileptic seizures), the
person behaves as if he has two separate spheres of consciousness. In
other words, neither half of the brain knows what the other is up to.

Now, you're probably aware that the left side of the brain generally
controls the functions of the right side of the body (e.g., movement)

and the right side of the brain controls functions on the left side of the body. Sperry's studies of patients whose corpora callosa had been severed or severely damaged showed that when images were presented to the left eye (connected to right hemisphere), the patient would be unable to say the name of the object (using language centers in the left hemisphere), but was able to pick out a similar object with the left hand (right hemisphere).

Researchers Michael Gazzaniga and Joseph LeDoux discovered something even more intriguing in a split brain patient who had limited language facilities in his right hemisphere. When they asked him, "What do you want to do?" the left hemisphere replied "draftsman," but the right hemisphere (using Scrabble letters to communicate) said "automobile race."

Yes, the left and right hemispheres often have very different aspirations.

Let's take a look at the functions associated with each brain hemisphere...

LEFT BRAIN

- Facts rule
- Reality-based
- Logical
- Practical
- Sequential; time sequence processing
- Rational
- Analytical
- Detail oriented; looks at parts
- Objective
- Likes safety

- Verbal/language skills: words and language
- Order/pattern perception
- Comprehension
- Knowing
- Acknowledges
- Forms strategies
- Skilled movement
- Present and past
- Math and science
- Knows object names

RIGHT BRAIN

- Imagination rules
- Global, holistic processing, "big picture" oriented
- Fantasy-based
- Uses feeling to make decisions
- Expressing emotions
  "gets it" (i.e., meaning)
  believes
  appreciates
- Intuition — reading emotions
- Holistic
- Synthesizing
- Random
- Subjective
- Evaluates wholes
- Presents possibilities
- Impetuous, takes risks

- Processing symbols and images

- Understanding metaphors

- Copying of designs

- Shape discrimination; e.g. picking out a camouflaged object

- Spatial perception, understanding geometric properties

- Knows object function

- Present and future

- Reading faces

- Music

- Philosophy & religion

Our brains are incredibly plastic. In each of us, one hemisphere is naturally dominant, but experience and deliberate brain training can increase the capacity and contribution of one hemisphere or the other. Most people tend to have more highly developed left-brain functions, which makes it more natural to slip into a left-brain mode of thinking when learning, solving problems or making decisions.

Most of us have been conditioned from childhood to be left-brainers; that is, to let the left-brain mode of thinking control our view of the world and dominate our decisions. For starters, formal scholastic education tends to favor left-brain modes of thinking and diminish the value of right-brain thinking. Left-brain curricula focus on logical thinking, analysis, and accuracy. Right-brained curricula, on the other hand, focus on aesthetics, feeling, and creativity. How many of *your* K-12 classes were devoted to right brain curricula?

Here's how a too-left-brained approach gets you in trouble with brand-building…

Traditional business strategists tend to view brands from only one angle and with a narrow view. They are viewing the brand from the inside, looking out: Unique Selling Proposition, P & L statements, mission statements, business models, cost analyses, operational plans, etcetera. They rely on historical trends to guide future development. It is a natural tendency — most corporate functions are managed from the inside out, after all. And it is true that without left-brained oversight, businesses might function only in a fantasy-driven tomorrow, ignoring the (sometimes expensive) lessons of the past.

Branding, however, is far more complex than that. It is driven by forces such as perceptions and mind-share — emotions — which operate from the outside in. Successful branding depends on accurately interpreting these elusive indicators — plotting the why-factors of the customer's buying decision in addition to the what, the how and the where.

In this new world of emotional branding, we must find fresh, innovative ways to create emotional connections with customers — from mind to heart to gut. From the customer's conscious aspirations to the subconscious — emotion, instinct and intuition. Marketers must think like customers, and that requires guess what…? Emotion, instinct and intuition.

An authentic brand perspective must encompass a *whole* picture.

AUTHENTIC BRANDING REQUIRES WHOLE-BRAIN THINKING

The whole-brain thinker knows how to forge emotional relationships with customers, while never losing sight of the P & L statement.

Some of the most financially successful brands in the world — for example, Virgin Records and Apple Computer — are emotionally-driven experiences that reflect the core values of their CEOs. Virgin Records' Richard Branston and Apple's Steve Jobs are two of the most creative CEOs in the world, brand maestros who have discovered the secret of whole-brain thinking.

Here is a little-known secret: The best leaders are *creative leaders*. They have learned how to forge emotional connections with other humans in all their communications. They know how to build and maintain an emotional brand.

Whole-brain thinkers build sustainable brands because they're able to *invent* markets, instead of just analyzing and measuring existing markets and toiling to carve out a narrow niche for their brands.

Brand strategists must connect the world of business rationale to customer emotion. Customers demand personalization, innovation, and performance, thus authentic branding is both a business model and an emotional experience. But make no mistake: Emotion always trumps rationality. The consumer-driven economy is an emotionally driven economy; marketing to the masses has succumbed to marketing to one. Yes, personalization is the watchword — personalization that acknowledges cultural and all other psychographical differences that deeply influence customer aspirations and brand perception. Brands have, in essence, become cultural phenomena.

Sadly, many businesses don not think like customers during the brand-building process. It is all left-brain, all the time. Meanwhile, the customer makes buying decisions in a very right-brain way.

SPHERES OF CONSCIOUSNESS

BUSINESS SPHERE	**CUSTOMER SPHERE**
Sales forecasting & trend analysis	Subconscious desires
Market research, demographics	Emotional aspirations
Profit & loss projections	Life-impacting ideas
Cost accounting & analysis	Intuition, gut instincts
Mission statement	Sensory experiences
Operational/prod. calibration & analysis	Stimulating design

See the gap between these two spheres of consciousness?

An authentic brand bridges this gap by appealing to mind and heart and gut. It isn't all about feelings. Emotion does have a relationship with reason: *Emotion results from an evaluation of what something means to you personally.* No personal meaning, no emotion. An authentic brand holds personal meaning for the customer, whether they consciously realize it or not.

AUTHENTIC BRANDS ARE HOLISTIC BRANDS

Holism is the theory that living matter or reality is made up of organic or unified wholes that are greater than the simple sum of their parts. If you complain to a psychotherapist that you are experiencing insomnia, loss of appetite and lack of energy, a competent psychotherapist will not diagnose depression without first making sure that there is not a physiological explanation for your symptoms. If you go to an internist complaining of these symptoms, a competent internist will not rule out the possibility of depression. In the medical world, symptoms cannot be viewed in a vacuum.

This holism holds true for authentic brands and the corporate cultures from which they emerge. In successful companies, creative people are free to create, but auditors are hovering in the background to make sure that the creative keeps at least one foot planted on the ground. And that whole-brain balance will ultimately be reflected in the success of the brand.

A holistic approach builds a better brand.

Here is an example of the left and right brain working in tandem on what would traditionally be thought of as a creative project. Imagine that you are doing a painting. Before you start painting, you try to visualize the final painting in your mind (right brain, contemplating the whole). Then you begin to develop the painting… choosing elements, textures, colors, placing shadows and highlights (right brain, working on various aspects simultaneously), but at the same time your left brain is critically analyzing each element…is that shadow realistic? Is the perspective correct? Is composition or depth of field off? Too much happening in the background? Your logical, analytical left brain is actually checking up on your right brain's "unfettered creativity," making mathematical calculations, doing "reality checks"… and finally perhaps asking: will anyone buy this painting? Does it have commercial value?

Sound like some brand strategy sessions you've attended?

Authentic brands are holistic in that authenticity is maintained across all touchpoints, throughout the three phases of brand-building:

- Master plan (Business Strategy, Market Strategy, Brand Strategy)
- Execution strategy
- Long-term brand management

A holistic approach to branding adds value and meaning to the brand, emotional fulfillment for the customer, and adds laser focus to brand strategy and execution. Holism helps ensure clear positioning that unifies both employees and stakeholders at every level, giving them purpose, pride, direction and motivation.

A holistic approach ensures brand sustainability, long-term value and equity.

WHICH KIND OF SMARTS DO *YOU* HAVE?

There are many kinds of smarts, but few (if any) of us excels at *everything*. That is why it is crucial for brand-builders to surround themselves with people who have complementary smarts. Brand managers, for example, who tend to focus too heavily on the rational, business and structural aspects of a brand must surround themselves with people who have a knack for aesthetics, creativity, engaging the consumer and stimulating an emotional response — even if that means retaining an outside branding firm.

Most contemporary neuroscientists support the idea of Multiple Intelligences. Developmental psychologist Howard Gardner proposed that each of us possesses at least nine measurable intelligences. Gardner believes that Multiple Intelligences include at least twenty-five additional sub-intelligences; for example, the domain of music might include such fundamentals as playing music, singing, writing musical scores, conducting, critiquing, and appreciating music, as well as the ability to perceive and execute tonality, harmony, rhythm.

The Multiple Intelligences fall into three broad categories: *object-related, object-free and person-related.*

Object-related forms of intelligence are controlled and shaped by the objects that we encounter and interact with in out environments. Object-free intelligences are not shaped by the physical world; they're dependent on systems such as language and music — cognitive and auditory systems. Person-related intelligences are related to our skills in interacting with other humans.

Which of these intelligences is your strong suit?

OBJECT-FREE INTELLIGENCES

1. Verbal-Linguistic. (Edgar Allan Poe, Franz Kafka, E.E. Cummings, Dr. Seuss, a.k.a. Theodore Geisel) These individuals have the ability to think in words, and to use language to express and appreciate complex meanings (e.g., authors, poets, journalists, speakers, and newscasters). Uses both the auditory and visual mode of perception. Verbal-Linguistics love learning new words and have high comprehension levels. They understand the order and meaning of words in both speech and writing, and know how to properly use language; they also tend to be precise in expressing themselves. They tend to "get" the socio-cultural nuances of language, including idioms, plays on words, and linguistically-based humor. Verbal-Linguistics enjoy creative writing, storytelling, reading, vocabulary, poetry, verbal debate, impromptu and formal speaking, word games, humor, journaling.

2. Musical (Bob Dylan, Wolfgang A. Mozart, Igor Stravinsky) Primarily uses the Auditory mode of sensory perception. These individuals are sensitive to pitch, melody, rhythm, vibration and tone. (e.g., composers, conductors, musicians, critics, instrument makers, and sensitive listeners). Musical intelligence is reflected in a propensity for: rhythmic and tonal patterns, vocal sounds and tones (including singing, humming and whistling), musical composition and creation, percussion vibrations, environmental sounds, instrumental sounds. These individuals are typically sensitive to sounds in the environment, such as the chirp of a cricket, rain on the roof, traffic noise. They can often reproduce melodies or rhythm patterns after only hearing them once, and may be skilled at mimicking sounds, language accents, or speech patterns.

OBJECT-RELATED INTELLIGENCES

3. Logical-Mathematical (Albert Einstein, Charles Darwin, Marie Curie, Jonas Salk, Jean Piaget) Primarily uses the visual mode of sensory perception. Logical-mathematical intelligence is the capacity to calculate, quantify, consider propositions and hypotheses, and carry out complex mathematical operations. Logical-mathematical strengths might be reflected in these abilities: problem-solving, outlining, deciphering codes, number sequences, abstract symbols and formulas, graphical organization, forcing relationships, identifying syllogisms and patterns. Logical-mathematically inclined people tend to think more conceptually and abstractly and are often able to see patterns and relationships that others miss. They are systematic and organized, and always have a logical rationale for everything. Scientists, mathematicians, accountants, engineers, and computer programmers are examples of people who demonstrate strong logical-mathematical intelligence.

4. Visual/Spatial-Mechanical (Pablo Picasso, Frank Lloyd Wright, Claude Monet, I.M. Pei, Walt Disney) Primarily uses the visual mode of sensory perception. These individuals have the capacity to think two- and three-dimensionally, "to think in pictures," perceive both external and internal imagery; recreate, transform, or modify images; navigate oneself and objects through space; to produce or decode graphical information. This intelligence represents the knowledge that occurs through the shapes, images, patterns, designs, and textures that we see, but also includes images conjured inside the mind. Visual/Spatial-Mechanical intelligence is found in, for example, pilots, sailors, sculptors, painters, and architects. These individuals are acutely aware of object, shapes, colors, textures, and patterns in the environment around them. They excel in imagination, painting, sculpting, drawing/illustrating, cartooning, mind-mapping, guided imagery, pretending, jigsaw puzzles, designing color schemes and patterns.

5. Bodily-Kinesthetic (Tiger Woods, Michael Jordan, Orson Welles, Jim Henson, Harpo Marx) Primarily uses the Kinesthetic/Tactile mode of perception, including touch, softness, slipperiness, twisting, jumping. Includes the capacity to manipulate objects and finely hone physical skills (e.g., athletes, dancers, actors, surgeons, and craftspeople). This intelligence is "learning by doing," often interacting with other intelligences such as musical (e.g., guitarists or violinists who fine-tune finger dexterity). These individuals might excel in inventing things, role playing, physical gestures and body language, dancing, martial arts, dramatic acting, mime, physical exercise and sports.

6. Naturalist (Charles Darwin, John James Audobon) Sensitivity to the environment; the ability to observe, understand and organize patterns in the natural environment. Naturalist intelligence is evidenced in the way we relate to our surroundings and the role each aspect of our surroundings play (e.g., molecular biologists, homeopaths naturopaths, oceanographers, geologists, meteorologists, astronomers). Naturalists are sensitive to seasonal or even daily changes (e.g., weather patterns) and are adept at distinguishing nuances between large numbers of similar objects. Naturalists traits include: classifying plants and animals, observing nature and environmental changes in general, sensitivity to animal behaviors , animal training skills, knowledge of gardening and growth cycles.

PERSON-RELATED INTELLIGENCES

7. Interpersonal-Social (Eleanor Roosevelt, Bill Clinton, Ronald Reagan, Mahatma Ghandi, Martin Luther King, Jr.) Interpersonal intelligence is the capacity to understand others, interpret their behavior and interact with them effectively (e.g., politicians, teachers, social workers, and actors). Interpersonal intelligence draws on a range of perception modalities, including visual, auditory, tactile and even olfaction and gustation (smell and taste). Individuals with high interpersonal intelligence learn though interaction. They're adept at giving and receiving feedback, intuiting others' feelings and motives, communicating one-to-one, participating in cooperative and collaborative team endeavors. These individuals are empathetic, tend to have lots of friends and are skilled in conflict resolution and mediation. They're often skilled at working out the best way to forge emotional connections with customers.

8. Intrapersonal-Self-Knowledge (Dalai Lama, Sigmund Freud, Deepak Chopra) Self-awareness and introspectiveness; the ability to construct an accurate perception of oneself and use that knowledge to plan and direct one's life (e.g., theologians, psychologists, philosophers, mediators). Individuals with high intrapersonal intelligence have strong concentration skills and they engage in silent reflection, and "centering" practices, mindfulness practices, metacognition techniques, higher-order reasoning, complex guided imagery, deep emotional processing, deep thinking. Intrapersonals are intuitive, self-reflective and self-aware, thus tend to be in tune with their inner feelings, values, beliefs, and aspirations. Their self-reflectiveness allows them to step outside of themselves and contemplate the meaning and purpose of their own lives — emotions, values, beliefs and aspirations. Intrapersonals are intrinsically motivated and do not need external rewards. They often like to work alone; they are generally self-confident and have definite and well-thought out opinions. They often provide creative wisdom and insight to others.

9. Existentialist (Dalai Lama, Jean-Paul Sartre, Soren A. Kierkegaard) Existential intelligence is the ability to be sensitive to, or have the capacity for, conceptualizing or tackling deep, complex questions about human existence, such as: Why am I here? Are there other universes? Is there life on other planets? What is consciousness? Where do we go when we die? Do animals go to heaven when they die? Is there any such thing as ghosts?

Existentialists are often described as wondering smart, cosmic smart, spiritually smart, or metaphysically intelligent. Existential intelligence may be seen in children who appear to have "old souls" or a sixth sense. Since neuroscientists can't quite definitively pinpoint the exact biological seat of spiritual wonder or cosmic awareness, existential intelligence is perhaps the most speculative of the Multiple Intelligences. Existentialism has no known locus in the brain, as do the other intelligences.

Psychologist Lawrence W. Sherman, Ph.D. has proposed a tenth intelligence that has relevance for some brands:

10. Gustatory/Olfactory Intelligence (Julia Childs, Coco Chanel) These individuals have a special sensitivity to chemicals, especially those associated with taste and scent (e.g., master chefs, perfumers, and vintners). They have an amazing capacity for discriminating between tastes and aromas, detecting blends of herbs and spices and perceiving grades of sweetness, saltiness, and acidity.

Contrary to the narrow range of abilities that standard IQ tests measure, Gardner's theory offers an expanded portrait of what it means to be human. And each of these intelligences can be developed and expanded in all of us.

Studies show that performance and appreciation of the arts enlarges cognitive capacities. Arts-motivated children develop attention skills and strategies for memory retrieval that applies to other subject areas.

Specific brain improvements linked to arts training include:

- Performing artists develop sustained attention and are highly motivated.
- Music training is linked to the ability to manipulate information in both working and long-term memory.
- Music practice is linked to geometrical representation skills.
- Acting training improves memory and semantic skills
- Learning to dance strengthens the neural substrates that support the organization of complex actions.

• Music training is linked to reading acquisition, phonological awareness and sequence learning.

And there is a bonus: The arts create a more enjoyable planet to live on.

HOW WE MAKE DECISIONS: Emotion, Intuition and Brand Strategy

THE LENS
The left-brain thinker and the right-brain thinker might analyze the same research data and see two totally different opportunities. Why? There may be a stark contrast between the colors of the lens through which each of them views the customer's brand experience.

Your lens colors your worldview and determines how you experience every aspect of life — from the way you experience a sunset to every strategic brand decision you make. One person may view a customer profile through a purely logical lens; another may view the same profile through a purely creative lens. One person may be optimistic; the other somewhat cynical. Someone who believes that opportunity exists in every market will view customer brand expectation differently from someone whose lens is clouded by fear of loss, or fear of being wrong.

Someone who believes that all decisions must be based on facts, figures, and rational thought will view brand-building differently from someone who understands that humans are not always rational beings, especially when it comes to how they make purchase decisions. How else can one explain the success of the Pet Rock? Who among us, after all, really *needs* to have a rock for a pet?

History — experience — installs an emotional filter between our perceptions and new experiences. This filter stores education, culture, psychological predispositions and emotional energy, creating a context for how we process information. Past and future events no longer exist as physical reality; the only "reality" is our memories of and feelings about those events. The filter collects new thoughts and emotions daily.

All new information flows into the mind through this filter. All decisions flow out through this filter. For both the brand strategist and the customer.

The customer's emotional experience is the most important component of the brand experience, and part of a larger symmetry: The branding strategist's ability to process each element of brand strategy, execution and management on an emotional level will be critical to forging a successful bond with the customer.

Gender is a lens, and authentic brand-building takes into account the gender differences between men and women.

Men and women are wired differently, neurologically speaking, and the wiring has a significant influence on buying behaviors. fMRI (functional Magnetic Resonance Imaging) brain scans show that women have nearly four times more neural connections across the corpus callosum than men. That is why women are better multi-taskers than men are. A woman's corpus callosum is more permeable than a man's — information can flow faster and more efficiently between the left and right hemispheres. Women are simply better equipped to transfer and link data from one side of the brain to the other.

It is also why women, in general, tend to be more naturally articulate, verbally fluent, perceptive and intuitive than men. Women are much more affected emotionally by ordinary language than men. The female brain can develop a wider perspective in thought processing, and respond to nuances in body language, tone of voice, and other non-verbal clues. Reaction time is generally slower in women, but accuracy is higher.

Should our modern neurological understanding of how the human brain works influence how brands educate and communicate with men and women? The answer is a resounding yes.

This is the decade of the brain. And thanks to fMRI, we can now peer into a person's brain and actually observe a person having a thought in real-time. Scientific neuroimaging research (known as neuromarketing in the marketing context) will ultimately have a dramatic influence on the decisions that marketers and brand strategists make because it allows them to pinpoint specifically what emotionally resonates with a customer. We can, for example, determine whether smokers respond to an anti-smoking PSA. Or show a 30-second spot debuting a new car brand and monitor levels of activity in brain areas associated with excitement and reward.

Neuromarketing can help us gauge true customer preferences and chart the brain activity that leads to brand choices. Which of these movie trailers will attract the most filmgoers? Or why, when a person prefers Pepsi's taste during a blind taste test, do they still buy Coca-Cola?

fMRI is the great lie detector: it can show us how people *really* feel, instead of our having to rely on them to tell us the truth in a focus group or opinion poll.

MOTIVATION REQUIRES EMOTIONAL EDUCATION

Researchers have now identified the brain circuitry responsible for reward-motivated learning — the brain's motivation station. Brain-scan studies show that we are far more likely to remember "high-value experiences" than "low-value experiences." Reward-related regions of the brain's emotion-processing mesolimbic region actually "alert" the learning- and memory-related hippocampus in the medial temporal lobe (MTL) to form a memory. In other words, an event, such as an enjoyable brand experience, interacts with the person's expectations and motivation to influence future experiences.

The mesolimbic circuit is activated when we even *anticipate* having a high-value experience. The brain actually prepares in advance to filter incoming information, rather than simply reacting to the world. Customers are *anticipating and hoping* for a brand experience that meets their expectations, and when they do, their brain circuitry gets excited and kicks into a motivational gear. They want to do something about it. They want to buy.

Emotions trigger background feelings, which come in an infinite variety of shades such as well-being, optimism, enthusiasm, cheerfulness, anxiety, melancholy, calmness, edginess. We are not always consciously aware of our background feelings because they're usually subtle. But subtle though they are, they can have a profound influence on our decisions and our behavior — and often in sneaky, imperceptible ways.

We rarely notice ourselves *knowing*. In fact, it is often beneficial to not notice background noise. We would drive ourselves crazy reflecting upon every tiny thought we have in the course of a day's time! Perhaps that is why the "default" is set to OFF.

But customer purchase decisions are directly influenced by these background feelings. Successful brands influence these background feelings in a positive and intentional way. Successful brand-builders ultimately come to see customer feelings, impulses and behavioral patterns as market data, which must be analyzed and calibrated just like a P & L statement.

THIN SLICES: CUSTOMER INTUITION AND THE SNAP JUDGMENT

How quickly does a customer make a buying decision? More often than not, much quicker than we imagine — even for expensive purchases. That's because the decision is about more than money. And sometimes because the decision was probably already made on some level. The customer had been thinking about buying that Ferrari and was just waiting for one more thing to tip the scale. That thing was *emotion*.

The left brain was calculating the cost, resale value and how much money you have, while the right brain was visualizing how great it would feel to zoom down the road with the wind in your hair and the sun at your back and envious passersby wishing they were you.

We have been conditioned to believe that the quality of a decision is directly correlated to the amount of time and effort that went into making it. But snap decisions — underpinned by intuition — can be every bit as sound as cautious as deliberate decisions underpinned by months of rational analysis.

The adaptive unconscious is the human sphere of consciousness that "leaps to conclusions." Now, the adaptive unconscious is not to be confused with the murky, conflicted unconscious, which harbors our desires, memories and fantasies. No, the adaptive unconscious can quietly — and with astonishing speed — analyze a tonnage of data; for example, the tons of data that today's consumer must process in comparing products.

The human mind is capable of flying on autopilot for many intellectually sophisticated tasks. The adaptive unconscious can size up the world, warn us of fraud or inauthenticity, set goals for us, and make efficient, sophisticated choices — all in the blink of an eye.

I want the longer-life battery, even though it's more expensive.

I choose Duracell because they always last longer.

We can make up our minds in seconds — nanoseconds even. And once we have reached a conclusion, we resist changing our minds. That is one reason it's so difficult in many markets to overtake the brand category leader. Customers made up their minds years ago about that brand, and they are resistant to change. That's good news for you, if you happen to be the brand leader. If you are not, you have got some innovating and differentiating to do.

Psychologists use the phrase "thin slicing" to describe the human ability to analyze and make sense of complex situations based on the thinnest slice of experience. A thin-slicer makes a quick decision about a new product from his cumulative wisdom about thousands of other products. Years of experience can be distilled to a single snap judgement. In other words, this customer is not, in fact, making a decision in the blink of an eye. It just seems like it.

This thin-slicing ability is *intuition*. Intuition is a slippery idea that often appears to defy conventional wisdom. Often we do not know where our first impressions come from, or exactly what they mean, so we do not trust them. Taking intuition seriously means we'd have to acknowledge that subtle influences can transform — even undermine — the power of our unconscious. We like to think we are more purely rational in our decision-making than that, of course. We are not, not necessarily.

In a brand strategist's world, good decision-making is a balance between deliberate and instinctive thinking. With experience and extensive knowledge of your customer, you may discover that you need very little new information to intuit the underlying signature of a complex trend. In fact, sometimes we take *too much* information into account when weighing a brand decision, instead of trusting our intuition — relating to the customer as one human to another.

Design visionaries, for example, can completely revolutionize a brand (and the profit picture) with one product. But convincing corporate left-brained thinkers that this innovative new design is The Next Great Thing is often a hard row to hoe.

Let's say that your market research reveals that customers don not want you to add any additional features to your Widget X10. But you have got an industrious product designer who builds a subtle, recessed handle into Widget X10's case, making Widget X10 easier to carry — encouraging customers to carry it. Guess what? It's a hit, customers love it. And it turns Widget X into the category leader inside six months. What happened? Customers didn't know they wanted portability.

Customers very often don not know what they want until you create it. That is why, in doing research, it is important to look for the ways in which design connects to emotions. Creativity should lead research, not the other way around. Research should emerge naturally from inspired ideas.

It is not enough to simply document that a thing works or how it works. You must find out *why* it works. Most revolutionary business innovations — and innovative brand identities — were inspired by a question that began with "What if...?" What-if questions spark the imagination and shake up perspectives.

The simple What-If question is one of the most powerful business resources you can employ. Ask enough What-if questions and you will eventually work your way to an innovative solution. And do not forget to ask: "What if we could build a brand that everybody falls in love with?" That is how you know you are on the right track.

Leonardo da Vinci used to hold his paintings to a mirror and view them in reverse. This technique, he said, made the painting seem as if were painted by someone else, which made him better able to judge its faults.

Reversal is a simple, but effective problem-solving technique. It is an old trick, but it works with thoughts, ideas, philosophies, and objects. If it's black, paint it white. If it is right side up, flip it upside down. Reverse your logo. Reverse the flow of traffic entering your store. Reverse your package design, Reverse your website Home Page.

Good product design, and good decision-making in general, is often about reducing a problem to its simplest elements. Even the most complex, vexing problems have an identifiable, underlying pattern. It is easy, ironically, to make something complex. But it's difficult to make something simple.

The unconscious is not a mystical force. It is an environment that we can monitor and educate. In *Blink: The Power of Thinking Without Thinking,* Malcolm Gladwell summarized that potential like this: "Every moment — every blink — is composed of a series of discrete moving parts, and every one of those parts offers an opportunity for intervention, for reform, and for correction."

Become a better user of your brain — your *whole* brain — and you will become a better brand strategist and strategic business manager.

Rivalry in the marketplace will only grow more fiercer. Whole-brain branding may ultimately be the difference between the successful brand and the *former* brand.

(3)

From Napkin Idea to Authentic Master Strategy
PART I

A brand must stand for something. And that something must be clear, in order to be perceived as authentic. What will you stand for?

Your goal is to create a brand so authentic that it would difficult to duplicate.

Perhaps you are beginning this branding journey with an idea scribbled on a napkin. Or perhaps your goal is to resurrect or revitalize a failing brand. Either way, you begin the process by developing an Authentic Master Strategy™ (AMS) that will guide you in building, executing and managing the brand. An AMS gives meaning and focus to your organization, and pride and purpose to your brand.

An AMS is more than simply organizing the functional benefits of your product. An AMS digs deeper, mapping out an overall blueprint for your core competence, target markets and brand identity — from your organization's intrinsic core values and culture to the brand's public personality and emotional appeal. Your master strategy will set the stage for successful execution of all the elements, as well as long-term management of the brand.

Your branding must embody the essence of your company. What do you stand for? What is your brand promise? Can you identify company values that customers can share? How will customers experience your brand? How will your employees experience your organization's culture? How will your brand experience differentiate you from all other competitors?

Your AMS must fill in all these blanks, or you will find it increasingly difficult to compete in the 21st Century marketplace.

Your job is to make people love your brand.

THE MODERN BRAND: BUILDING TO COMPETE

The cost of a brand failure is high, often to the tune of millions — even billions — of dollars.

New brands are hatched and sent forth into the marketplace every day. Most of them will fail within a year or two —perhaps even months. And each year, a certain number of known and established 20th Century brands will die. At the time of death, many of them will still have brand awareness and even decent market share, but they are no longer connected to the 21st Century customer, whose contract demands an emotional bond.

Why do brands fail?

Brands can fail for many reasons, but one big one is that they were not built to compete in the new economy. Often, strategists (business, marketing, and branding) are looking back, instead of looking ahead. They waste time imitating what has been done before, instead of innovating and differentiating; instead of investing time, thought and money in a forward-looking master brand strategy… in authenticity, originality, reality; instead of investing long-term in inventive product design, technologies and service touchpoints that benefit their customers and society at large.

If it's already been done, don't do it. Do something else. And design that something else to appeal to today's customer, not yesterday's.

Let's take a look at how 20th Century brand strategy compares to 21st Century brand strategy…

20th CENTURY BRAND STRATEGY

- Vision: Making money

- Business Model: Reinforce familiar ideas

- Customer's Profile: Demographics

- Sales: Push marketing models

- Profits: Familiar revenue streams

21st CENTURY BRAND STRATEGY

- Vision: Making the world a better place

- Business Model: Innovation and differentiation

- Customer's Profile: Psychographics

- Sales: Pull-through models, personalization and customizing

- Profits: Multiple revenue streams

In the old economy, the corporate vision focused on making money, money, money. Well, vision is still about making money, of course, but with a twist: make money while making the world a better place. Business philanthropy, for example, has become a hugely successful strategic public relations model. Through charitable giving to philanthropic causes, businesses can communicate their humanity, generate publicity and goodwill, and attach new value to their brands. Strategic philanthropy builds brands and a better society.

Iconic Hollywood actor Paul Newman will be remembered for many things, and one of them will be the philanthropic business model he established with his Newman's Own brand. He was an astute marketer, who, in some ways, may have set the pace for business philanthropy. Newman disliked the phrase "cause marketing." He was driven by a sense of doing what's right and sharing his abundance with others.

Companies all over the globe are linking their brands to philanthropy.

Tide, for example, donates a portion of the proceeds from sales of Yellow Cap Tide to disaster victims, "mixing hope with the normal load."

Brands must be good citizens of the world. Brand citizenship is here to stay. In our emotionally driven marketplace, consumers respond to brand cultures that are committed to contributing to society and making the world a better place. The new definition of brand leadership may ultimately require attributes of humane leadership.

In the 21st Century, innovation and differentiation are critical to a brand's success. Messaging has become less about tradition and the *familiar,* and more about the future and *innovation.* And customer psychographics will be more important to your strategic planning than demographics. Psychographics can provide more pure-octane motivational power to drive a brand than demographics ever will. Psychographics provide *inspiration.*

What is the difference between psychographics and demographics? Psychographics are the intangible customer attributes: inspirations, aspirations, motivational forces, lifestyle. Demographics are the old tangible attributes that give us a surface understanding of the customer, but never quite tell us enough; for example, age, gender, ethnicity, socioeconomic status. Knowing that a prospect is a 35-year old Hispanic female who has the money to buy your product does not tell you how to motivate her to, or whether she is even a viable prospect. But if you have a deeper understanding of what she wants out of life, what delights and inspires her, you have a much better shot at forging both an emotional and intellectual connection with her.

In the new economy, push marketing is dead — replaced by *pull-through marketing.* The Fuller Brush man does not show up on your doorstep any more, hawking his wares. Instead, *consumers* decide what they want through education, and go after it.

The economy has shifted from a factory-based, production-driven, capability-driven model to a consumer-driven model that requires more innovative and flexible branding. Speed to market has become a formidable competitive edge. For example, if a customer can not find a product they want at their local grocer and asks the grocer to order it, the customer has just customized her shopping experience, and changed her grocer's inventory plan, to boot. Eventually, the store might stock the product on a regular basis to meet growing demand.

Note that demand is actually traveling backwards: from the consumer to the retailer to distributor to packer to producer. The grocer is no longer setting demand, nor is the producer. The customer is.

Custom-ers demand *custom*-ized brand experiences. Perhaps the term "customer" has finally laid claim to the full meaning it should have possessed all along.

Marketing, sales and revenue models have shifted in the past couple of decades. The advertising model is struggling; the public relations model is thriving. The pull-through effect, for example, is often the result of brand awareness, which glowing publicity can help generate.

Years ago, public relations were considered secondary to advertising. PR people existed to reinforce advertising; they essentially looked for crafty ways to communicate the brand's slogan or tagline. But today's brands are built with publicity and maintained with advertising, not the other way around. What other people say about your brand is far more powerful than what you say about it.

In the old economy, we trolled familiar revenue streams for profits. In the new economy, we generate multiple revenue streams (ideally, as many of them passive and running on autopilot as possible) and we use technology and innovative thinking to do it.

AUTHENTICITY STARTS WITH YOUR BRAND'S PHILOSOPHY, VALUES AND VISION

The genetic makeup of your brand will be defined by your Authentic DNA Code™. That Code is comprised of two strands:

Core Business Strategy + Core Brand Strategy

Authenticity emerges from your Authentic DNA code. Your DNA code is critical in defining the core of your business model and your brand values, from which you'll build out all other business and brand attributes.

Remember, your strategy must connect the dots between your brand values, brand identity and brand image. In other words, you must align the values of your company and products with the brand identity you hatch and send out into the world and the customer's perception of that identity.

Brand alignment matters. That means your AMS must link your business strategy to your brand strategy (also known as customer experience). The whole-company culture must unite and align all the organization's behaviors behind a clear authentic brand.

Build an Authentic Master Strategy, and an authentic brand will become a self-fulfilling prophecy.

> STRATEGY SESSION:

An authentic brand starts with an organization's CEO and trickles down. Your brand philosophy will be part and parcel of your corporate culture.

1. Define your CEO's Authentic Brand Philosophy. Brand philosophy is the source of your brand. Your brand philosophy will be the GPS that guides your business in every endeavor. Brand philosophy is the heart and soul imprinted on your company's brand core. Authenticity naturally emerges from corporate culture. It is holistic, the very essence of how your entire organization operates on a daily basis — in the marketplace, in the boardroom.

Your brand philosophy will reflect your brand's personal values and principles through your brand's infancy, defining your corporate consciousness from an early age. As your brand grows up, you can never lose sight of your brand philosophy. It will always preserve your brand's essence and maintain brand authenticity.

EXERCISE:

Draft a Brand Philosophy statement. *Our Brand Philosophy is…*

Imagine your brand as people, places or things and answer these questions…

A. What are your brand's passions in life?

B. What is your brand's natural and intrinsic "gift?"

C. What are the values that guide your brand culture's daily life?

D. What are the core beliefs that your brand will take a firm stance on?

E. What lifestyle does your brand represent?

2. Define your CEO's Authentic Core Brand Values. Identify 3-4 core corporate values: This is your brand essence. (Example: *integrity, quality, and passion*) Your core values should be encapsulated in three or four words; they must be simple, powerful and memorable. Your core values should be so indigenous to the brand core that, if they vaporized so would the company and its culture.

EXERCISE:

List 3 to 4 core values and describe each. Answering the following questions will help you pinpoint authentic values.

A. What values are so indigenous to your brand that if they vaporized, your brand image would disappear?

B. What values does your brand consistently adhere to in the face of all barriers and threats?

C. What core values does your brand culture value from the inside out and from the outside in?

3. Define the Authentic Brand Vision. All your strategic decisions must align with your brand vision. Vision should be so compelling that it inspires all stakeholders to participate in building the brand culture — from employees, customers and shareholders to manufacturers, buyers, sales reps and store clerks.

Like all species in nature, all companies — and all brands — must continually adapt to their environments. But core values remain the company's backbone. These unchanging values are your *brand vision*. This vision will continue to navigate you through trouble waters and inspire you while on your journey. Brand vision is what you intend to deliver.

For example, in the 2008 presidential campaign, Barack Obama (who is nothing, if not a brand!) wanted to communicate *hope, optimism and change.* He summed up his vision with the slogan: *Yes, We Can.* Three simple words said it all.

EXERCISE:

Draft a Brand Vision statement. *Our Brand Vision is...*

Answering these questions will help you pinpoint and refine your vision...

A. What are the results based on your business committed?

1. Look into the future 100 years out... what legacy do you want your brand to leave behind on this planet?

2. Specifically, what people, places and/or things are empowered by your brand's existence?

3. What is the driving force behind your vision?

B. What are your business goals and its mission.

    1. If your vision became reality, what would transform on this planet?

    2. What strategic partners would your brand vision attract?

    3. What potential threats may stand in the way of realizing your vision?

BRAND ARCHITECTURE: BUILDING THE HOUSE

The marketplace is comprised of humans who come from many cultures and have different needs, desires, and goals. You must clearly define your Brand Architecture at the outset in order to sustain value, growth and equity, and to profitably manage the masterbrand and any sub-brands you spin off for the long term.

A focused brand architecture plan will:

- Clearly identify and profile your customer aspirations
- Strengthen brand loyalty within your existing customer base
- Create speed into new or existing markets
- Strengthen and enhance sales strategy goals
- Protect the brand, enhancing both marketing and legal strength; identify and develop intellectual property assets, patents and trade secrets that build brand equity and value
- Help you identify and create profitable brand extensions and line extensions without diluting the brand

In general, there are two models of brand architecture:

    1. House of Brands

    2. Branded House

General Motors is a house of brands; the General Motors company brand is the masterbrand, the parent corporation, and its 2009 subbrands include Cadillac, Pontiac, Buick, Chevrolet, Saturn, Saab, GMC, Hummer.

In some houses of brands, the sub-brands should dominate the master-brand. It is more important for the public to connect with the sub-brand because the subbrand must differentiate itself against its competitors.

While the original core GM brands look different from each other, some would argue that they are, as a whole, less differentiated from other competitive vehicles in their price category (e.g., Ford-Mercury, Chrysler). Cadillac, General Motors' prestige brand, is the exception.

BMW, on the other hand, is a branded house. All sub-brands support the branded house. All say: *I'm a* BMW. And all models are differentiated from all other vehicles. With BMW, the subbrands become trade dress. They sport a similar appearance; for example, the trademark kidney stone grill. When BMW launched the dramatic rear end redesign, they redesigned all models.

Your masterbrand vision and values must be carefully developed, and each subbrand must conform to the masterbrand's values. BMW's branded house strategy is powerful because prospects can identify the vehicle as a BMW on sight, which boosts the value not only of each subbrand, but of the entire BMW masterbrand. Prospects understand what the car stands for.

Ultimately, all the BMW subbrands become aspirations for customers. If you're driving a 300-series, you may aspire to bump up to a 500-series BMW. BMW customers choose BMW because of how the car makes them feel; this is an important extension of aspiration. They can imagine themselves behind the wheel.

In addition to strategizing the emotional connection of a brand, it is important to consider the financial and legal ramifications when you create brands. For example, the house of brands architecture tends to create more revenue streams and offer better exit strategies. Selling one sub-brand does not necessarily impact the others. You can keep the brands that are successful and sell or liquidate the ones that are not. If one fails, it usually does not take the others down. You can generally isolate and contain the damage, thus preserving the rest of your brand portfolio.

Richard Branson's Virgin house of brands is a good example. The masterbrand is Virgin; sub-brands include Virgin Records, Virgin Airlines, Virgin Drinks, Virgin Limousine, Virgin Mobile, and that is just for starters. The companies were established as separate brands and separate legal entities; each has a separate legal firewall and financial firewall.

Consider General Mills sibling strategy for its family of brands. General Mills owns cereals such as: Cheerios, Cocoa Puffs, Lucky Charms, Total, Wheaties, Trix, and Raisin Nut Bran. But General Mills also owns separately branded companies such as Betty Crocker and Pillsbury. Consumers care more about the specific cereals than the company name. Cocoa Puffs lovers could care less that those little chocolatey puffs are made by General Mills. Most of them probably do not know. And it does not influence their buying decision one way or the other.

If you build a strong house of brands, you can dominate a market for years. General Mills avoided giving their brands a "family look." Each brand looks distinctly different. General Mills also owns Olive Garden and Red Lobster. Instead of trying to stretch their brand equity in cereals into the Italian and seafood restaurants market (can you imagine General Mills Restaurant?), they created completely different — and individually distinct — brands.

Sub-branding must be done carefully. If you are thinking about creating a sub-brand for an already successful brand, make sure you are not chasing the market instead of shoring up the brand, or you will end up diluting the brand. Clothing designers are notoriously susceptible to expanding lines in a fashion, so to speak, that ultimately dilutes the brand. Consider a clothing designer who manages to successfully imprint a brand in high-end women's fashion, then decides to parlay that brand success into new markets and new lines... high-end men's fash-

ions, then children's fashions, then a "value line"of women's fashions...
and on and on until they have finally diluted the brand to the point
where no one understands what the brand stands for anymore.

The expansions looked great on paper. New markets! More revenue
streams! But they were abstract concepts that had no basis in reality.

Think like the customer.

Invest the time on the front end to devise a master strategy that will
work for the long haul. Undoing a branding mess can be tricky. It is not
as simple as swapping out a logo. Nor can you simply change the names
of companies and products mid-stream. Brand confusion is one of the
worst sins you can commit.

Some general brand architecture guidelines to keep in mind…

- Customers buy brands, not companies. Brand names should
  almost always take priority over company names. When people
  discuss purchases, they seldom repeat the company name. They
  are more inclined to use the product's brand name. Ever heard
  anyone say, "I just bought a brand new General Motors Cadillac
  STS..."? Building strong product brands is especially critical in
  a competitive market where the product's features are narrowly
  defined, and targeted to a narrow psychographic.

- A company name is just a company name, unless the company
  name is being used as a brand. The company manufactures,
  develops and owns the product. It is not the product itself. For
  example, Adobe, Inc. is not Acrobat. Adobe, Inc. develops many
  software packages, one of which happens to be Acrobat.

- If it is not critical for the product to imprint as its own brand,
  focus on branding the company as opposed to the product.

Let these rules guide you when building a family of brands...

- Sibling portfolios should revolve around a common product area.

- Devise unique — not *similar* — brand names and brand messages.

- Distinguish siblings by a single attribute, such as usage or experience level of your target market; for example: *beginner, intermediate, advanced or industrial, professional, personal* use.

- Lay down the law about sibling rivalry. Maintain strict distinctions between sibling brands. If you are segmenting by price, do not let the price levels bleed into each other. If you're segmenting by experience level, do not let beginner products slide toward advanced products.

- Don't create a new sibling unless you can not create a new category. For example, do not simply create a sibling brand because your competitor has a product in that niche. Instead, create a new niche.

> STRATEGY SESSION

EXERCISE:

Define your Brand Architecture Plan.

A. Clearly define your company's product and/or services

B. Think long-term: Decide whether you will be a house of brands or a branded house

C. Define your company's business revenue model

WHAT'S YOUR MESSAGE?

Your core brand message is the key message that your company will communicate to every audience. All other messages that emanate from your company will be offshoots of your core message. The more closely your core message reflects the reality of your brand experience and the reason your brand exists, the more effective your brand message will be, both within your organization and to the outside world.

The authentic core brand message forges a swift and powerful connection with customers. Your message should be simple, concise, and easy to remember. It must strike a chord intellectually and emotionally — it *must* strike the heart, gut or mind, or a combination of these three zones.

Consider the strike zones for these brands:

Harley Davidson: gut

Victoria's Secret: heart

Intel: mind

Apple: mind, heart and gut

Is your message masculine, feminine, or gender-neutral? Are you Virginia Slims or Marlboro? Both are cigarettes, but they target very different demographics and psychographics.

Are you Mountain Dew or Pepsi? Mountain Dew strikes the extreme sports chord. Pepsi strikes the team sports chord.

> STRATEGY SESSION:

1. What difference will your brand make among people's lifestyles? How will your brand change the marketplace? (1 – 2 sentences)

2. What is the current perception of your brand in the customer's mind and heart? (Interview at least 10 people)

3. List 7 beliefs about your brand in the marketplace and the contrasting realities. How many of the beliefs match the realities? On a scale to 1 to 10 (10 being best) how far is your brand from being authentic?

EXERCISE:

Draft your Core Brand Message. (20 words or less)

Then answer these questions...

1. Is your core message authentic? In other words, it is real?

2. Is it unique from your competition in your industry?

3. Is your core message clear, concise and easy to remember?

Authentic brands are concise, memorable, differentiated and true.

MAKING THE PROMISE

An authentic brand makes a promise that will be honored, time and time again.

That promise is a contract between you and the customer. Delivering on your promise builds a foundation of trust; not delivering on your promise is a breach of contract.

There can be no disconnect between the promise and the experience. Delivery on your promise means meeting the customer's expectations and aspirations. A great product leads to a great emotional experience, and that experience leads to another. And another. And another.

Your brand promise should represent the core values of your company, and differentiate your brand from its competitors. Your promise can not fall into the sameness of "just making more money." An authentic promise always has much higher aspirations.

CASE VIGNETTE

In the wake of the telecommunications revolution of the 1990s, many reseller companies rose, and almost as many fell. Customers had too many suppliers to choose from, most of which failed to offer attentive service and accountability. Telecommunications provider ATI was founded as a counterpoint to this trend, building its business on low price points, backed by extraordinarily high-quality service for every customer. However, the challenge for ATI was that the old marketing approach was no longer working so well. ATI employees and agents viewed the company's branding as uninspiring. Prospective customers no longer saw ATI as unique. Market tastes had changed. But ATI's marketing approach had not. Nothing new was at work here.

It was time to reposition the brand and the marketing approach. HOW Creative worked with ATI to convey a brand promise of stability and superior service in an unstable industry. ATI's entire brand identity system was revitalized and rebranded, which included integrating every single touchpoint — brand icon, website, tradeshow displays, brochures, ads and more.

The repositioning focused on ATI's sales agents, who were, after all, the "boots on the ground," the folks closest to ATI's customers. An innovative "Wealth of Reasons" incentive program was created, demonstrating to agents that ATI really cared about them. In addition to receiving standard commissions, agents could do something extra for their families through this premium incentive program that awarded points for hitting certain sales levels — points that could be applied toward merchandise and other incentives (such as vacation trips and even a Porsche).

The result? The Wealth Program succeeded on every level, both promoting sales and generating agent goodwill and loyalty, which dramatically improved agent retention and recruitment. ATI literally redefined the reseller concept in the telecom industry. And as a result, ATI is one of the few telecom resellers that thrived. Today, it serves a large commercial and wholesale customer base, backed by the highest quality service.

EXERCISE:

Answer these questions, thinking like the customer:

1. What is the customer's ambition or goal?
2. List customer barriers/objections to buying your brand, product or service
3. What is the solution for overcoming each barrier? Describe solutions for each barrier that would eliminate or solve the customer's problems and enable them to achieve their ambition.

Now, draft an irresistible Brand Promise. *We promise to…*

WHO'S YOUR TARGET?

Know thy customer. This old adage can never be overemphasized.

In today's segmented marketplace, it's become even more critical to pinpoint true targeted customer segments, and understand the aspirations of each class of customer.

We interpret words and images according to our cultural experience and education. These psychographic influences add context and emotional nuance to our brand experiences and influence the way we make buying decisions.

Let's say you are offering a money-making opportunity… is your prospect likely to be more interested in achieving prestige and status, or achieving great wealth? At first glance, it might seem that these two profiles are the same, but they're not. People are always motivated by one factor more than the other. Identifying such narrow distinctions is key to creating a brand experience that motivates prospects to buy. Understanding these distinctions will guide all your communications with prospects and help you develop a touchpoint plan that has the ring of authenticity.

You must understand how your customer thinks…and feels. And why.

What is your prospect's education? Profession? Social status? Socioeconomic status. Are they WWII, baby boomers, Gen X, Gen Y, Gen Z?

Are your prospects busy, demanding, discriminating? Urban, cosmopolitan, or rural and laid-back? Agrarian or industrial? Manufacturing or engineering-minded? Pragmatists or dreamers?

What is your prospect's vocabulary? Would your prospect be more likely to respond to (and trust) casual or formal language?

Customer profiling helps you get a handle on your prospect's goals, aspirations, and motivation. Let's say, for example, your product is health-related. Is your target prospect seeking cure or prevention? Are they desperate to find a cure? Are they looking for an alt-product?

To pinpoint a clear customer profile, you must understand generational differences between:

Baby Boomers (1946-1964)

Generation X (1965-1976)

Generation Y (1977-1994)

Generation Z (1995-present)

Each generation has very different views of itself and responds to very different stimuli.

To the Boomers, generation is iconic, it is about US — *we* are a defining generation in the history of the world. To Gen X, generation is *individualistic*, it is about *I* — we are *rebels*. To Gen Y, generation is *philosophical*, it is about all — we have a *conscience*.

As children of the turbulent and mercurial Flower Power, Rock 'N Rolling 1960s, Baby Boomers grew up unsure of who they are; they just know they are not in Leave It To Beaver Land anymore. In the new millennium, they seek leisure, financial security, wealth and perks; they're worried about aging and health issues. They long to fulfill aspirations. They emotionally respond to realistic ideas, icons and pioneers, religion, symbols of achievement. Many still view the world in race-divided and gender-divided terms. They are largely tech fearful.

Gen X is a generation of individuals and customizing. They respond to reflections of themselves in marketing, nostalgia (as long as it's hip), and messages of spirituality. Gen X is pessimistic and concerned with health and well-being. They are tech-proficient; they like alternative music and sports and emotionally respond to multi-ethnic and uni-sex concepts. They seek fame and fortune. They like style and luxury goods, and respond to celebrity idols and reality TV. They want to be inspired, and they seek tools that help maintain their chosen lifestyle from books to seminars.

Gen Y has a sense of community, loves interactivity and lives in a global culture. Gen Y is tech savvy, heavily engaged in social networking, sharing real-time information, TiVo, DVR, cell phones. Gen Y is a generation on the move; they stay in constant contact with each other; they register *.mobi* domain names. Gen Y is fun, optimistic, and marketing savvy. They like extreme sports, multisensory, multimessage and multimedia experiences. They like learning, new ideas and philosophic brands, and respond to cues of sexuality, mysticism, talent with messages — especially if the messenging acknowledges that they're smart.

And what about Gen Z? Gen Z will be the uber-connected multi-tasker. These kids grew up on TVs, computers, video games, iPods, cell phones, digital phones, DVD and DVR recorders — all of which are being rolled into convergence devices. Technology years are like dog years — technology advances by leaps and bounds. Bandwidth gets wider and wider and faster and faster. Everything wired is becoming wireless. 4G is just the beginning for this ultra-mobile generation. Electronic media devices abound and marketers will have to dramatically shift our paradigms of communication with this generation.

Media is no longer time-and place-based and message delivery is user-controlled. It will be a pull-marketing world. The Gen Z media revolution is shaking up both popular culture and brand strategies.

BENEFITS, FEATURES OR ADVANTAGES. As you profile your customer, align customer attributes with your product or service attributes: *features, benefits and advantages*. What is the difference between these three?

Features are specific product attributes — what the product does. Benefits are the ways you are going to make your customer's life better. Advantages could be the reasons they should buy your product over a competitor's, or an edge your product will give them over their competitors. With some products and services, benefits and advantages may be fundamentally the same.

Making distinctions between features, benefits and advantages is an important organizational step. It will help you prioritize product attributes and structure your promotional materials for each medium.

> STRATEGY SESSION:

EXERCISE:

Define your Authentic Customer Profile, including both demographics and psychographics.

The goal of this exercise is to identify every characteristic of your customer, no matter how seemingly small. Sometimes small is big. Sometimes the smallest characteristic can lead you to your differentiating attribute.

Answer these questions from your customer's perspective:

1. What is your arena?

    A. Broad category first (e.g., B2B or B2C)

    B. Possible subcategories. (e.g., Marketing & Advertising? Health & Fitness? Fun & Recreation?)

C. Niches. Are you targeting one niche or multiple? (e.g., Dieters? Or dieters and people health-conscious about what they eat?)

2. Pinpoint your customer's demographic: age, gender, education, profession, socioeconomic factors, etc.

3. Identify your customer's psychographics

4. Identify features and benefits sought by your customer

   A. List the functional (intellectually-driven) benefits and features (e.g., comfort, highest quality, specific solution for a problem)

   B. List the emotional (Heart-and Gut-driven) benefits and features

5. What customer needs does your product or service fulfill? Increased speed, productivity and efficiency? Convenience? Increased business? Shorter sell-through cycles?

6. Identify the perks your customer will appreciate, or perhaps even demand. (e.g., the feeling of "being treated special," convenience, 24-hour support)

From Napkin Idea to Authentic Master Strategy
PART II: DIFFERENTIATION

An authentic brand is not necessarily the first to market; it is the brand that comes first to the customer's mind. The one that comes to mind is the one that stands apart from all the others. An authentic brand owns a differentiating attribute.

A differentiated brand is a huge and immediate competitive edge. In fact, it is your strongest marketing guarantee. And it is your strongest legal protection, should a competitor try to cash in on your success.

You can never lose sight of the fact that your customer always has a choice, even if your product or service has no competition. They can choose to buy a completely different kind of product. They can choose to buy nothing. They always have a choice.

That choice can be you.

Whether consciously or unconsciously, the prospect who is pondering whether or not to buy your product or service is essentially asking the question: *Why choose this one?* Your differentiating attribute is the answer to that question.

WHATEVER HAPPENED TO THE USP?

In the old economy, we built brands around the USP (Unique Selling Proposition). But guess what? Customers are not interested in what you have to sell anymore. They are willing to buy, but they do not want to be sold to. They want to be inspired. They are buying an *experience*.

Consumers tune out traditional selling techniques. No one listens to the sales spiel from the used car salesman who's chasing them all over the car lot. Talk about a negative brand experience! And that's why tonality is so important in all your communications. Tonality can either repel or compel. If they're not listening to you, you can't establish an emotional connection or inspire them to buy.

Rosser Reeves introduced us to the USP in his 1960 book *Reality In Advertising*. Reeves, who saw brand as "a product with a plus," laid out a rigorous three-part definition for the USP:

1. Each advertisement must make a proposition to the consumer. Not just words, not just product puffery, not just show-window advertising. Each advertisement must say to each reader: "Buy this product, and you will get this specific benefit."

2. The proposition must be one that the competition either cannot, or does not, offer. It must be unique — either a uniqueness of the brand or a claim not otherwise made in that particular field of advertising.

3. The proposition must be so strong that it can move the mass millions (i.e., to pull over new customers to your product.)

Reeves was not wrong. All these tenets are true. But consider how the world has changed since 1960. Consumers are far more cynical now than they were a half-century ago. Today's consumer demands more. More information. More innovation. More personalization. *How will this make my life better?*

The Product is what the customer thinks it is.

Marketers love to preach about the USP. Ironically, many of them do not seem to have one. Instead of communicating specific differentiating benefits, they will toss out vague benefits and attempt to make them *seem* specific. "You will earn $7,500 a week using my e-learning program!" A benefit which *sounds* specific, but does not differentiate the brand from a hundred others. Plus, it is a benefit that is probably impossible to guarantee. If you can not guarantee it, it is not a promise.

A brand is a promise, and it must deliver on that promise.

In today's marketplace, me-tooism is the predominant competitive force. Sad but true. Most companies imitate, in hopes of cashing in on their competitors' successes. But me-too products, are inherently undifferentiated. Guess what this means for you? That is right. It is a great time to innovate and differentiate!

If you are going to imitate, you had better count on having a ton of money to sink into promotion — or more to the point, out-promoting your competition. Microsoft is perhaps the most obvious example of this me-too breed of brands. Microsoft does not innovate, never has — despite advertising claims to the contrary. Microsoft copies its competitors, shamelessly. Or buys them out. Or failing all else, forces them out of business. Microsoft dominates not by being different, but by unleashing a rip tide of advertising money that drowns its rivals. Their differentiating attribute is monopoly. But no monopoly lasts forever. Just ask Ma Bell or AT&T.

You can not rely on your brand's USP anymore to close the sale. Every brand competing against yours claims to have a unique selling proposition. And you can not rely solely on your brand's past reputation. Your prospects do not care about yesterday. They demand to know what you've done for them lately. And what can you do for them right now. How will you make their lives better? Authentic branding always answers the question *How will this make my life better?*

Marketing today is not about selling. It is about *educating and how to.* With more brands than ever before, customers have more choices, thus more control. They determine what will make their life better, and which product is the right one to do it. You help them make that choice by connecting to them on an emotional level and educating them about the product, the service, the industry… and why *your* product.

Winning mindshare and heartshare is critical to gaining long-term equity, profits and growth. You win mindshare and heartshare by clearly communicating to your prospects what they should know and care about with respect to your product or service, and why they should trust your brand. Trust + clear communication (brand promise + education) is the ultimate shortcut to closing the sale. To accomplish this feat, you must go beyond the USP to the UPP (Unique Purchase Proposition) and brand promise. You must communicate exactly how you will fulfill your customers's expectations.

In the new economy, a brand becomes a unique purchase proposition through education. Crafting your UPP requires focusing on the subtle and sometimes overlooked *why*-factors of a particular buying decision. For example, when Curad wanted to take on the formidable Band-Aid brand in the adhesive bandages market, they launched a line of bandages with cartoon characters printed on them. Kids, who comprise the largest consumer base of bandage users, loved them. They were practically a fashion statement, a collectible. It was a small but innovative differentiating attribute that directly, emotionally appealed to the hearts and minds of the target consumer. As a result, Curad stole a chunk of the bandage market from brand leader Band-Aid.

The unique purchase proposition is essentially a *unique value proposition* that forges both an intellectual and emotional bond with the customer. Product benefits still matter, of course. If you want (need) to buy a watch that is waterproof, you are not likely to buy a watch that is not water-proof.

But the customer perception of *value* extends beyond the functional benefits of a product, or even the service and support a company offers. The perception of value can be enhanced by many attributes of your organization, such as your brand's personality, your industry reputation, product and promotional design, and even a compelling brand symbol.

You want people to fall in love with your brand, and bond with it through trust.

The Japanese term *otaku* has been used in the context of brand appeal. Otaku describes a drive that is more compelling than a hobby but a little less than an obsession. A craving? A compulsion? The distinctions probably are not important. What is important is that it drives customers to your brand.

For example, thousands of people camp out overnight at a concert ticket outlet so they will be first in line the next morning when the tickets go on sale. Or thousands of people camp out overnight at an Apple Store to guarantee that they will get iPhones the second they become available. (This actually happened, all across the country.) This is a customer with otaku.

These customers knew that Apple was not selling only a limited number of iPhones. When the first batch ran out, Apple would make more, exactly like the original batch, and customers knew it. Yet these overnight campers were willing to go to great lengths to get an iPhone, the "first" iPhone — *immediately.* Today's consumer often seeks instant gratification, especially the consumer with otaku.

Can you inspire otaku? Ask yourself these questions:

- Does my brand convey instantly the unique purchase proposition in today's market climate?
- Does my brand provoke instant recall and recognition in the customer's heart and mind?

If you answered yes to both questions, you're on your way to achieving customer otaku.

> **STRATEGY SESSION:**

EXERCISE:

Draft a unique value proposition statement. Write a simple, clear statement (1-2 sentences) about your brand that tells your customer why your brand is the choice for them. The statement should contain a concise and memorable phrase that answers your prospect's always-implicit question: *Why should I choose you over your competitors?*

ARE YOU DIFFERENT? YOU'D BETTER BE.

Anything can be differentiated.

Part of the trick is to create your difference, and use that difference to drive your benefit message. Use your difference to set up your unique value proposition. In a crowded category, differences usually need to be dramatic, simple and easy to grasp. Even if that means oversimplifying your message, distilling your difference to one attribute.

Do not try to tell the whole story. Focus less on communicating the attributes that your competitors can claim, and more on what they *can not* claim that you can. Focus on one differentiating idea that you can drive home, again and again. The most effective attributes are simple and focused on customer benefit, regardless of how complex the product or market is.

For example, Visa's share of the credit card market shot up more than 50% after taking ownership of the word "everywhere" in their "Visa is everywhere" campaign. Volvo owns *safety*. FedEx owns *overnight delivery*. Zippo owns *windproof lighter.*

Some people will not like your distinctive new brand, your product, or you. Be prepared for it. It comes with the territory. People are always suspicious of the new, the different, the revolutionary, the maverick, the big thinker. This is one of the main reasons that major companies often shy away from creating distinctive products and building distinctive brand identities. They are afraid of not being liked — or more to the point — afraid of being criticized. But guess what? No brand is universally loved by everybody. If you stand out, you will be criticized. But criticism does not equate to failure.

Being safe is risky. Being boring is risky. In today's crowded marketplace, it is hard to survive if you do not stand out. Being scrutinized — even criticized — is not the worst thing that can happen to you. Being invisible is the worst thing that can happen to you.

Some organizations believe that differentiated branding takes courage. The irony is, it takes courage to launch an undifferentiated brand. You are pitching a brand out into the marketplace with your fingers crossed, hoping no one will notice that there is no difference between your brand and your competitors' brands.

These days, many companies are conserving capital, playing it safe, eliminating risk (or so they believe) every way they can. Guess what this means? That's right. It is a great time to innovate and differentiate! Create a new brand category. That is how you beat the market leaders.

LAY OF THE LAND: YOUR POSITION IN THE BRANDSCAPE

Are you Macy's, Nordstrom's, or Tiffany's? Are you Wal-mart, K-Mart, or Target?

Your brand must stand for something. One of the most important aspects of differentiation is brand positioning — how a brand is positioned against its competitors in the marketplace, as well as its sibling brands. The clearer your position, the more likely you are to stand out as a billboard in the consumer's mind. Along with clear brand identity, and positioning, direction and motivation for all your stakeholders — from your customer service reps and product designers to customers and shareholders.

Over time, many companies who create a successful brand feel pressured to grow the business, expand the line, expand the product to target new market segments. "Modernizing" brand positioning must be done thoughtfully. It is always easier than people think to destroy — or at least dilute — the identity that made the brand successful to begin with. As soon as you start presenting the brand as something other than what it is known for, you weaken your differentiation, undermine your brand identity and shift the customer's image perception.

If you change an existing product to appeal to a new market, you can end up chasing away your old customers. You may just be chasing a trend, instead of revitalizing the brand. Veering off your brand course to imitate your competitors just so you can nab some of their customers is almost certain to fail. Those customers already belong to them. Target different ones.

But whatever you do, do not cling to an old brand positioning that has become (or becoming) obsolete. Better to kill the obsolete brand and launch a new brand.

It is always tempting to just point out an obvious product attribute and simply claim superiority. It rarely works. No one will believe you. Consumers, let's face it, have become far too cynical for that.

You can not build a unique purchase proposition around a difference that doesn't exist. The hard cold truth is that there is little differentiation among brands in most markets. Why? Because the most frequently deployed differentiation tactics do not work, or at least, rarely work. That's why there are so few true market leaders! And one reason so many brands ultimately go belly up.

Brands who fail to create and communicate a differentiating attribute usually end up resorting to using price as a differentiating attribute. Price is not a differentiating attribute. Your competitors can always slash their prices overnight, or offer more bang for the same buck. This is certainly more true today than ever before, thanks to the instant notification channels — the Internet and 24-hour media. Where would that leave you? You're suddenly the brand that not only costs more, and has no justifiable (differentiating) reason for it.

To pinpoint a differentiating idea in a market where there is competition (which is most markets), or at least perceived competition (again, most of them), you are seeking the thing that separates you from the pack. Simple and obvious, right? Not necessarily.

Your idea of your product's differentiating attribute may not be shared by your prospects. It is amazing how far out of sync the customer perceptions of a brand and perceptions of the company who owns the brand often are. One of the likely culprits behind this lack of synchronicity is that the company's brand identity has not been properly built, executed and managed. There is a disconnect between the customer's brand perception (brand image) and the brand identity the company intended to communicate.

> STRATEGY SESSION:

EXERCISE:

Draft your Brand Position statement:

Our authentic brand positioning is the exclusive [category specifier] _____ that has the [unique and differentiating attribute of] _____.

DIFFERENTIATION TACTICS

Differentiation enhances a brand's authenticity.

There are hundreds of narrow, specific ways to differentiate a brand. The best way, of course, is to actually *be* different. In other words, own an authentic differentiating attribute, a product (or company/culture) difference that you can present and prove. Claiming a difference with no proof of one is just a claim, nothing more. A claim has no brand value.

The attribute you decide to own does not have to be specifically related to the product itself. Your company philosophy may be your difference. Your heritage. Your Vision. Your brand personality. Your total brand experience.

Some differentiation tactics are more effective than others. Some of the most common ones are the ones you should avoid…

DIFFERENTIATION TACTICS TO AVOID

PRICE. Differentiating by price is a temptation for many, as if price were the only factor in buying decisions. Buyer psychology is far more complex than that.

It is hard to differentiate successfully a brand by price. For starters, if price is the central focus of your message, you already will not be perceived as unique. Lower pricing can, in fact, actually run counter-intuitive to differentiation. Truth is, people will generally pay a little more for better quality and — this is important — they typically *expect to.*

In some markets, lowest price can make you look desperate. Customers will wonder what is wrong with your product, and whether you are about to go bankrupt. Pricing impacts brand perception. Your price is a reflection of your brand's value in the marketplace. It certainly indicates how much *you* think your product is worth.

It is possible to differentiate with low-price strategies in mass-merchandising, where giant markdowns are much easier to make profitable. The trouble is, what's to keep your competitor from doing the same thing? And there goes your edge.

In today's crowded, competitive marketplace, a price-only differentiation strategy is usually not enough. There are better strategies.

QUALITY. Actually providing authentically superior quality will strengthen your brand over time. But quality is an *expected* attribute, not a differentiating attribute. Customers expect the product they buy from you not to fall apart. Since no one believes you when you claim superior quality (everyone makes this claim!), you can not count on claims of superior quality to differentiate you from the competition. After all, no competitor sells their brand as the *low-quality* product. (Not intentionally, at least.)

Now, this does not mean that you should not try to differentiate your product's quality from your competitors. You should. Just don't count on that being perceived as a differentiating attribute.

One technique is to say quality without ever saying it. Instead, use code-words such as...

blue-ribbon, champion, top-flight caliber, stature, virtue, worth

respected, discriminating, distinguished

SATISFACTION. Customer satisfaction is subject to the same rules as quality. Satisfaction is expected, not optional. Dissatisfied customers expect refunds. This does not mean that you should not guarantee satisfaction — you should. But doing so will not make you unique. Pretty much everybody offers satisfaction-or-money-back guarantees, and many of them even stand behind it.

A savvier, more demanding consumer base has raised the bar for brands. Today's marketer must be hold onto existing customers while landing new customers. Selling quality and satisfaction are rarely enough anymore. In most niches, it is a buyer's market. All the more reason to focus on authentic differentiating attributes. These days you can only successfully differentiate your brand with quality or satisfaction strategies when your competition is dumb enough to let you.

So, let's explore effective differentiation tactics...

BEING FIRST

Being first means you are the *original.* Being first makes everyone else copycats. Being first is instant and automatic differentiation. The first company knew a secret and was innovative and perseverant enough to develop it and bring it to market.

First says tested and proven, and can suggest that you are the brand leader. Customers are more likely to believe what you have to say when you have leadership credentials.

Why is Coca-Cola The Real Thing? Because Coca-Cola invented colas.

And guess what? Coke is still The Real Thing. Firsts often stay first because it is hard to overtake the leader. It is hard to overtake the leader because differentiation becomes more difficult when you weren't there first. Seconds, thirds and fourths can not own the same differentiating attributes already owned by the first. Those are already taken.

Now, there are some inherent risks to being first. You can never predict with certainty the marketshare or mindshare that a new attribute can own, and it is possible to misjudge the market. Some products take time to catch on — that's a risk that requires you to be well-capitalized in order to hang in there. For example, VCRs were actually introduced in 1956, but did not catch on until 1975. Phone answering machines were around in the late 1950s, but did not catch on until the 1980s.

Sometimes being first is about simply studying the market, predicting trends and kicking into gear before your rivals do. Have an original idea and have it first. If you design a good product, market it well and fend off the copycats, you will be successful.

HERITAGE

Companies with a long history have a built-in psychological advantage: Prospects are more comfortable buying the brand that has been around a long time. Heritage can go a long way toward eliminating a buyer's perception of risk. Heritage says leadership. Heritage equals brand equity.

Buying products from a company with a history allows a customer to actually participate in the company's legacy. Consider family-owned businesses such as In & Out Burger, Hardy Jewelry. Some customers will flock to them just because they have been hearing about them for years from others who enjoyed the brand experience.

There is more than one way to qualify for the heritage differentiation tactic. For example, your company might be young, but your product may have a legacy. Let's say you bake and sell gourmet cookies made from the recipe you inherited from your great Aunt Gertie. Tell Aunt Gertie's story… how she immigrated to the United States from Germany in the cargo hold of a steamer, how she always wore colorful gingham shirtwaist dresses, how you remember sitting on her wrap-around porch in the summertime as a youngster munching oatmeal raisin cookies, the great care she took in concocting her cookie recipes.

Tell your history, but only if an interesting one.

A family business is always a good differentiation strategy, especially in today's marketplace of humongous, impersonal superstores. Heritage can make brands not only different, but *better.* Customers tend to assume that they will receive a higher level of personal care from family businesses because the owners are more personally involved. Customers implicitly understand that the family name, after all, is on the line. Family businesses tend to rank a few rungs up on the trust ladder.

GEOGRAPHICS

Where you come from can provide heritage credentials and a differentiating attribute. Does your brand hail from a region that is noted for something?

Consider these examples of geographically related heritage credentials:

New Orleans: jazz and Cajun cuisine

Germans: automobile engineering

Italians: beautiful apparel and shoe design

Swiss: finely crafted timepieces

The Caribbean: tropical sun, white sand, gorgeous blue-green water

Las Vegas, Nevada: casinos and entertainment

Hawaii: aloha, hospitality

Nashville, Tennessee: country music

Omaha, Nebraska: beef/steaks

PREFERENCE

In general, people buy what they think they should have. *Should* is often influenced by what *others* think they should have. Humans are social creatures, and they are more comfortable and confident in making choices when they have Social Proof. Often, we decide that the correct behavior is what we see others doing, so we mimic their behavior. Trusting the social evidence, we figure, means we are less likely to make a mistake. If so many others believe something is true, it must be.

Preference is one of the easiest differentiation strategies to build. It is also one of the most effective. Customer preferences come in many flavors. The broadest type of preference is a *market preference.* Communicating market preference means communicating to prospects what others think is the right choice. The beer breweries, for example, are notorious for citing market preferences. *Preferred by discriminating beer lovers.* If you are a discriminating beer lover, you will choose our beer.

Preferences abound in the marketplace, and branding strategists aggressively target a preference by constructing a brand identity and message around it. It works. And it becomes its own self-perpetuating brand image throughout the life of the brand.

Cowboys wear Wranglers, not Levi's.

Harley Davidson owners are rugged and all-American. (Can you imagine a Hell's Angel riding a Honda?) Harley Davidson even owns a patent on the Harley sound — that is how critical and valuable a differentiating attribute they believed the rumble of that engine to be.

Speedo is about function and performance; it is for the serious athlete. Quicksilver is about form and fashion; it is for the athlete who wants to look cool and hip.

Shop the Internet in your pajamas, instead of schlepping to a brick and mortar store…click a couple of buttons and merchandise magically shows up on your doorstep.

Do not trust a 2-D photo on a website? Shop a real brick and mortar store and experience the merchandise up close and personal.

- Fresh foods versus frozen foods.
- Fresh foods with no "additives" versus processed foods.
- Lulu for yoga vs. JC Penney.
- Hollister Ranch vs. Volcom.
- Pink vs. Victoria's Secret.
- TapouT vs. Nike.

PROCESS

Is there something unique about your manufacturing process, seasoning process, curing process, delivery process? Sometimes a product can be differentiated by the way it was built. Software, hard goods, gourmet foods, bottled water... the strategy is the same for any product. If there is something about your process that differentiates your product, sell the process and explain why it matters.

Your process can even be mysterious. You can withhold secret ingredients and processes, as long as you reveal enough to prove your difference. If your competitors are offering cheaper and cheaper components and less and less bang for the buck, call them on it. Offer more. Offer better. And charge more.

If all the competing products are square, make yours round, then demonstrate why round is better. Maybe round fits more precisely. Maybe round is safer. Maybe round is easier or the hands to hold.

If your product is authentically innovative, that should be the foundation of your differentiation strategy. Or perhaps your process is innovative, thus making your product innovative. Perhaps your product or service adds a layer of innovation to boring technology.

In technical markets, focus on being *the next*, rather than being *the l atest* even if you have to obsolete your old products to do it. Next is not totally without risks. For one thing, Next must be *better*. No one will buy Next if it is worse, or less than its predecessor. Do not pretend to solve a problem that does not actually exist or is nothing more than a tiny glitch that no one is willing to discard their old tried and true product to fix. Do not make the mistake of trying to solve problems that people are not willing to pay to fix.

The Netflix brand is not only an example of differentiation by process, it is an innovative business model that revolutionized the DVD rental industry. Netflix pioneered the DVD rental model by delivering video rentals via mail or streamed to your computer or Netflix-ready device— the ultimate in convenience and efficiency. Place an order and receive videos the next day by mail, or instantly, if you are digitally-enabled. Mail order customers return videos by just slipping them into a postage pre-paid envelope. No more schleps to the video store to rent or return videos ala the old Blockbuster model.

In the new economy, process is often about technological innovation. Consider the story of Nintendo's Wii game console…

In creating the Wii, with its innovative Wii remote controller, Nintendo created an aspiration that actually motivated customers to buy, whipping the likes of Sony (Playstation 3) and Microsoft (Xbox) in the process. Nintendo ultimately exceeded its own original aspirations for the Wii brand's chosen category, expanding its reach into a much broader market.

Game consoles typically attract youngish males, but the Wii has proven to be addictive to people from such diverse demographics as elderly residents in nursing homes. Neuroscientists have used Wii as an intelligence-improving device in developmental learning studies. And most interestingly, with Brain Training for Adults, as a tool to reduce brain age and ward off the effects of dementia and Alzheimer's disease…

Brain Training, developed by Ryuta Kawashima, a prominent professor of neuroscience at Tohoku University, is a package of cerebral workouts targeted to grey gamers that may improve mental agility and even slow the onset of dementia and Alzheimer's disease. The player's "brain age" is determined as they complete puzzles, including reading literary classics aloud, simple arithmetic, drawing, and responding rapidly to deceptively easy teasers using voice-recognition software.

Researchers claim to have seen marked improvements in people with dementia who perform these simple mental tasks that require them to use the prefrontal cortex to restore brain function. Neuroimaging tests of various brain functions showed that the brain functions better when confronted with simple calculations than when multi-tasking during a conventional computer game.

The hope is that Alzheimer's patients who continue this learning therapy a few minutes each day may ultimately not have to take drugs to delay their symptoms. Brain Age-equipped consoles are even available in some Kyoto waiting rooms and hospital wards.

The game will not cure dementia, but it is a good form of mental stimulation. Perhaps more importantly, the fun and easy-to-use consoles help the elderly confront their fears of spending their twilight year's miserable and lonely without mental and physical well-being. The idea of training the brain instills hope.

Being good at computer games is no longer just a symbol of misspent youth. Nintendo, through technology and innovation has created a potentially important learning therapy tool, and in the process, contributed to an often-forgotten population, an instrument of hope.

In the new economy…

Technology + Innovation + Relevance + Value = Big Profits (And Authenticity)

The whole-brain brander knows how to build a brand bridge between fundamentals, innovation, creativity, technology, and return on investment.

Strive to set a new standard.

For example, here are some cases where HOW Creative worked with existing, known brands to innovate solutions that set new standards and further enhanced difference and authenticity…

- Fujitsu's first digital ad for national magazines *MacWorld* and *MacUser* innovatively combined and manipulated 14 separate photos into a single shot, garnering awards and attention and putting Fujitsu on the map in the removable disc market segment.

- Digital Wall Street Journal advertising helped position Claris FileMaker to ultimately dominate its market category.

- HOW Creative helped ABC networks pioneer a cost-effective offline computerized motion graphics presence for its Saturday morning programming, eliminating the need for costly, high-end online HAL and Henry video editing. ABC was the first to use offline algorithmic editing solutions. Not only did ABC save a fortune, they changed one aspect of television viewing forever.

- Royal Phillips Electronics CD-i its initial DVD movie campaign launch provided customers with superior and more sophisticated audio and video, and contributed to the obsoleting of all the old "pre-DVD" formats) and JVC's VHS and Sony's Beta cassettes format. DVD became an industry standard.

DESIGN & PACKAGING

Your difference can — and should — be executed across all your touchpoints… brand, company or product names, taglines, brand icon, customer service, design and packaging. Brilliant product design, graphic design and packaging can set you apart from the competition and make your brand the one that springs to mind first.

What is your competition doing? Do something else.

Design and color can help you sharpen and flavor your brand message. Color, for example, plays a key role in crafting a brand personality that evokes the response you desire, whether you need to convey excitement and energy, or comfort and reliability. Authentic brand identity has a color.

- Avis is red, Hertz is blue.

- UPS is brown, FedEx is purple and orange.

- IBM is blue, Apple is red.

- Coke is red, Pepsi is blue.

Design is always about more than the aesthetics. It is about the emotions good design evoke; that, after all, is how you forge that necessary emotional bond with the customer. Today's marketers must view their brands as more than commodities; they must see their brands as emotional design. Design-driven companies differentiate their brands and, often, revolutionize their industries.

The Mini Cooper, with its build-your-own, personalized marketing strategy is a great example of both design and packaging. Do you want the John Cooper Works? Or do you want the Hardtop, Clubman, Convertible… or perhaps the Hardtop S, Clubman S, Convertible S? Should we paint your Mini Chili Red, Pepper White, Midnight Black, Pure Silver, Dark Silver, Sparkling Silver, Mellow Yellow, British Racing Green, Laser Blue or Horizon Blue?

In the high-end bottled water market, Fiji has stolen market share from Evian by creating a distinctively sensual bottle design that is emotional and personal.

In Chapter 8, we will explore the impact of design on branding in depth and discuss strategies for innovating and differentiating through design.

> **STRATEGY SESSION:**

It is time for some competitive research. Whether your mission is to build a new brand or reposition an existing brand, these exercises will help you chart the right course.

EXERCISE:

1. What distinguishes you from your top 3 competitors? Chart your top

3 competitors and compare them to yours. Beside each competitor, list strengths, weaknesses, unique features, benefits, and emotions (from your customer's perspective).

2. List the unique attribute(s) of your brand. This attribute should make your brand unique in its market segment and differentiates your brand from its competitors. What does your product, service or company culture have that no one else's has? What can you own that no one else owns?

3. Based on the customer profile you created in the last chapter, what customer ambitions, emotions, and needs are your competitors not fulfilling?

4. Scope your competition's business model. Who are they targeting? What channels do they sell through? What is their delivery model?

5. Analyze how your competition presents their brand in the market-place.

   A. How are they positioning their products against other competitive offerings?

   B. What representations are they making?

6. Study both media and consumer reviews of competitors; conduct your own polls, if possible.

   A. What are the perceived strengths and weaknesses of each competitive product?

   B. Does the product positioning in the minds of customers match the positioning your competitors are aiming for? Once you can rank product attributes on a competitor-by-competitor basis, you'll know which competitor owns which attribute. Your goal is to own a different one.

7. Does perception align with reality? For each of your top 3 competitors, look for gaps between what they claim and what is actually true. Are they claiming features, benefits or advantages that their brand does not actually possess? (If so, that is an opportunity you can exploit.)

Strive to own the most important attribute in your category. Otherwise, you may be forever doomed to a smaller slice of the market. Whether you own the most important attribute or not, it's still better to be *different.*

But simply owning a strong differentiating attribute isn't enough. You have to communicate that difference. It's not possible to *over communicate* your difference. Reinforce your message again and again across all your touchpoints. Customer perceptions evolve through communication. Remember, you're fighting for mindshare. And marketing is a battle fought in the mind of the customer.

Great copy differentiates. A distinctive brand name differentiates. A unique, professional graphic look differentiates. Personality is perhaps the greatest differentiator of them all. Pair a compelling brand personality with an authentic differentiating attribute, and you've got an unbeatable combination.

From Napkin Idea to Authentic Master Strategy
PART III: PERSONALITY

An authentic brand has a personality. A spirit. A tone. A voice. It breathes, and evokes emotions.

Why is brand personality critical to brand identity? To succeed in the new economy, brands must build relationships with consumers and provoke an emotional response. A distinctive personality establishes a consistent brand positioning and cements the impression of your brand in the consumer's mind.

Personality is a powerful competitive advantage. In fact, it is one of the strongest lures a brand can offer. A brand must be bigger than a handful of attributes which can be imitated or surpassed by competitors. Personality is a powerful and sustainable competitive edge because it is very difficult to copy. Imitators will be seen as posers and imposters; hence, by definition, *inauthentic*. In fact, any competitor who attempts to copy your brand personality is effectively testifying to your originality and authenticity.

That is a good position to be in. An authentic brand is so original that it is impossible to duplicate.

WHAT IS BRAND PERSONALITY?

The personality component of brand identity encompasses the non-product-based, nonfunctional dimensions of the brand. Every brand can be described in terms of physical, functional or symbolic attributes.

But personality serves the symbolic aspects of your brand. Personality can even create a self-expressive role for consumers who become involved with your brand. Consider what happened with Levi jeans in the 1980s. Europeans and Russians were willing to pay big bucks to experience this all-American brand. And, of course, citizens in other countries take a big bite of America every time they eat at McDonald's, which now has 31,000 local restaurants in 118 countries.

Think of brand personality as the unique set of human personality traits that are applicable to and relevant for a brand. In other words, a brand's personality, at its core, parallels human personality.

Personality is an individual's way of being in the world. Personality usually has nothing to do with the cognitive aspects of a person's behavior (e.g., intelligence, ability, knowledge). Personality always revolves around the affective, emotional and dynamic aspects. And personality is experienced and evaluated by others on an emotional level.

Human personality is composed of traits or markers that are (as Freud would tell you) dynamic and cumulative, but, above all, durable and relatively stable over time. This is the same with brands. Brand personality must be a constellation of stable, persistent traits. Since brands are often personified by consumers (perceived as people), human personality descriptors (adjectives) can be used to describe brands.

In crafting your brand personality, it is important to remember that most buyers believe they know who they are as individuals, or, at least, they have carefully honed a certain self-image that they aspire to live up to, or pretend they live up to. Buyers tend to fall into clusters of people who share common self-images, worldviews, aspirations, attitudes, and belief systems.

I'm upwardly mobile, and the car I drive and clothes I wear should reflect that.

I believe in going green wherever I can.

I'm one of those early adopters who always buys the latest techno-gadget.

Life's short — let's party!

An authentic brand becomes a badge — a part of the customer's self. Does riding a Harley make you feel rugged? Does shopping at Tiffany's make you feel elegant, sophisticated and wealthy?

Once you understand the psychographics that motivate your target clusters, you will understand how to craft a brand personality that will appeal to them; that is, you will know how to connect with them on an emotional level.

Personality is the great differentiator. Personality traits can forge powerful symbolic associations in the brain. Take Southwest Airlines' TV commercials. Southwest used humor to differentiate; a flight attendant who cracks jokes with passengers lightens the heaviness of air travel, which, as we all know, can be annoying, frustrating, and anxiety-provoking. Virgin Airlines took a different approach, differentiating the brand as a luxury airline whose flights include such perks as TV screens and laptop connections for every seat.

Most of the other airlines blur together, an undifferentiated cacophony of price battles.

The handwriting is on the wall, certainly in retail. Undifferentiated, impersonal personality-less big-box retail stores are slowly dying. Small, personable, intimate boutiques are making a comeback. When low price is the only differentiator you have got going for you, you have destined for trouble.

Target differentiated its brand as "Mass with Class." Wal-Mart has continued to brand itself as featuring "everyday low prices" and the king of "rollbacks." They are taking a brand hit. In the past few years they have resorted to building new stores in higher socioeconomic neighborhoods, instead of sticking to their original marketing model. The result is that they've ended up embroiled in neighborhood zoning battles that effectively say: *We don't want you here. We don't want your ugly warehouse building or your traffic cluttering our neighborhood streets. We are anti-mass-market.*

An authentic brand has higher aspirations. An authentic brand creates and/or reflects a lifestyle — activities, interests, opinions. And always, of course, aligns with the customer's aspirations. Consider Apple's "Hi, I'm a Mac...", "And I'm a PC..." TV commercials, which literally turn brands into humans to convey the Apple Macintosh brand message, personality and overall attitude and core values of the respective brands.

Mac says, I'm hip and fun, easy to set up, loaded with (only cool) software, bug-free.

PC, on the other hand, laments his difficulty of use, propensity for crashing and contracting viruses, the fact that he is bloated with useless trial software.

Apple has been fundamentally consistent in expressing its fundamental core values since the 1980s, even when it was competing against IBM for hardware share. Apple (user-friendly innovation) versus IBM (traditional, reliable business solutions) The personality differences extended to brand icon colors: IBM (formal, dignified, authoritative blue); Apple (energetic, charismatic, playfully rebellious red).

Your brand personality will send messages about your brand values. Take a look at these core personality traits and the brands that made a deliberate decision to own them...

- Sincerity (Hallmark)
- Excitement (Ferrari)
- The Most Trusted Name in News (CNN)
- Cable Sports Network (ESPN)
- Sophistication (Tiffany's)
- Ruggedness (Coors Beer)
- All-American Outdoors Cowboy (Marlboro)
- Sexy female (Virginia Slims)

- Amped Energy (Red Bull)

- Competence (Weather Channel)

- Green/Environmentally Friendly (Toyota Prius)

- Green speed (Tessla)

- Civilized high performance (Aston Martin)

- Think Different (Apple)

- Think Small (Volkswagen Beetle)

- Safety (Volvo)

- Speed (Porsche)

- Efficiency (FedEx/Kinko's, now known as FedEx Office)

- Smart innovation (Intel)

- Make something great (Stanley)

- Saving lives (American Red Cross)

- Big and Strong (Caterpillar)

- Adventurous (Club Med)

- Hot girls and wings (Hooters)

BRAND CHARACTERS

Jolly Green Giant. Mr. Clean. Mr. Peanut. Aunt Jemimah. Ronald Mc-Donald. You can picture these characters and hear their voices, can't you? Of course, none of them actually exist. They're fiction. They are caricatures, portrayed by human actors, or animated cartoon characters.

Characters — personas — can be a great way to launch a product. Characters work because they humanize brands. But there is a trick to it: The persona must link the product to concepts that the public already understands. A well-crafted character is a symbol that communicates the essence of your brand.

Clever and authentic fictional characters can become your spokesperson, pitchperson, your stand-in. Truth is, they are more likely to be remembered than you. Fictional characters, for example, can be outlandish and exaggerated. They can get by with things you can't.

Some brands have been successful using real-life humans as brand characters; Kentucky Fried Chicken's Colonel Sanders, for example, successfully pitched his own products for decades. He aged with the brand, a familiar, white-haired avuncular figure who reminded you a little of Santa Claus. You believed he cared about the quality of the chicken he sold.

Characters fell out of favor for a while, but they are making a comeback. That's another great thing about fictional characters. They can vanish overnight and reemerge on your whim. In other words, as changing markets and marketing trends mandate. Mr. Peanut, Mr. Clean and the Jolly Green Giant, previously removed from service, are now back pitching. Nostalgia sells, particularly to older shoppers and people who are into retro chic. Nostalgic comebacks can be effective because they are emotional links to the past, and because something old reemerging becomes new again, a.k.a., differentiated.

BEWARE THE SYBIL EFFECT

Consistency is a critical attribute of authenticity. Consistent brands reach and connect with more people, and over time, build long-term loyalty and brand equity. Coca Cola, for example, is today what it was 20 years ago, and it has the brand equity and market cap to prove it.

It is important to craft a brand personality that is executable across all your touchpoints — now and for the long term. In other words, your personality must be expressible in various mediums. You want the brand-customer emotional bond to be reinforced each time a customer encounters one of your touchpoints — from their first glimpse of your brand icon on your product or packaging to your website's tone, design and content. Every touchpoint is an opportunity to amplify and exemplify your core personality traits.

Most brands in the marketplace suffer from Brand Identity Disorder, conveying splintered messages and multiple personalities. Sometimes the disorder can be traced back to faulty strategic planning; sometimes it is just the result of sloppy brand execution and management. Either way the brand image begins to disintegrate in the customer's mind.

Imagine how you would be received if you showed up at an important business meeting wearing an Armani suit and flip-flops. Your personality is not integrated. Your colleagues would not know what to think. They will wonder who in the world you've become. That also goes with brands. If your brand personality is not integrated, you are effectively sending alter personalities out into the world to tell your story. The result is too many voices and too many versions of your truth.

In the clinical world, such behavior might be diagnosed as Dissociative Identity Disorder or, as it's commonly referred to, Multiple Personality Disorder. (Remember Sybil, with her many alter personalities?) Dissociation is a disruption of the usually integrated functions of consciousness, memory, identity or perception — all of which are crucial to brand authenticity and brand strength.

Interestingly, the clinical symptoms of Multiple Personality Disorder align with the symptoms of dissociative brands...

- The patient (brand) has at least two distinctive identities or personality states. Each of those has its own relatively lasting pattern of sensing, thinking about and relating to self and environment.
- At least two of these personalities repeatedly assume control of the patient's (brand's) behavior.

Presenting multiple personalities is the epitome of inauthenticity. Customers do not know who they are dealing with. They do not understand what your company stands for. And guess what? They won't trust you. Humans are innately suspicious of inconsistency, especially when the source of that inconsistency is someone who wants to sell us something. Building a relationship has just become far more challenging, and your reach into the marketplace is likely to be shallow.

Your brand's personality can never be dissociated from your brand image. It *is* your brand image. In order to be perceived as authentic, your brand personality must be fully integrated with all other key elements of your brand identity, and tucked into each of your brand touchpoints. If your brand personality is spunky and witty, your corporate culture should be spunky and witty. Hire customer service representatives and field reps that are spunky and witty.

Ditto your website and all collateral materials...

LANGUAGE & PICTURES HAVE PERSONALITY, TOO

Every promotional venue — from websites and brochures to ads — has the opportunity to convert strangers to customers and set a tone (in voice and look and feel) that persuades people to believe the story you are telling; in other words, to earn their trust, and convince them that you are authentic.

Brand personality adds dimension to your brand, and sets both a sensory and narrative style for all your touchpoints. Personality emerges from many cues that surround the brand experience. Many variables influence brand personality... brand name, logo, celebrity endorsements, colors, shapes, music and sound effects, product packaging and promotional materials... and that's just for starters.

Personality always drills down to the language you use. A distinctive brand tone not only makes your copy more persuasive, it makes writing it much easier. Plus it makes it easier to write in a consistent tone groove.

The narrative voice in every communication should always conform to your brand tone. It does not work to have a cheerful brand name, a bright, friendly yellow logo and somber, brown copy.

Pick a voice that inspires and is compelling to your target audience. Then stick to it. Never, ever change it. You can bend it or stretch it a little, but never change it. If customers sense an identity split, they will not trust you. Consistent voice breeds trust; they know what to expect when they first hear the sound of your voice.

CDBaby.com' sales confirmation emails are a great example of brand communication you actually look forward to. It is a killer tone and personality touchpoint; and if you ever get one, it is a touchpoint you never forget...

> Your CDs have been gently taken from our CD Baby shelves with sterilized contamination-free gloves and placed onto a satin pillow. A team of 50 employees inspected your CDs and polished them to make sure they were in the best possible condition before mailing. Our packing specialist from Japan lit a candle and a hush fell over the crowd as he put your CDs into the finest gold-lined box that money can buy. We all had a wonderful celebration afterwards and the whole party marched down the street to the post office where the entire town of Por tland waved 'Bon Voyage!' to your package, on its way to you, in our private CD Baby jet on this day, Tuesday, June 18th. I hope you had a wonderful time shopping at CD Baby. We sure did. Your picture is on our wall as "Customer of the Year." We are all exhausted but can not wait for you to come back to CDBABY.COM!

CDBaby.com' confirmation emails are so fascinating that you actually read them. What a refreshing change from the usual boring Confirmation Email. When was the last time you actually read one of those?

Consider this Giorgio Armani website copy. Does this say Armani to you?

A NEW FORMAL DRESS CODE

There is a new, unexpected but deliberate disorder about this collection in that it refuses to recognize the hierarchy of dress. Here each piece can be combined democratically, added or subtracted that defines the edgy contemporary. Glossy fabrics create contrasts with chunky matt wool; a featherweight mesh layered over printed patterns blurs the edges. A headscarf tied like a turban appears to unravel on the nape, the generous cape style coat seem to melt round the body: aesthetics and shapes have been chosen to update the somewhat theatrical impact of Eighties-style fashion.

Take a look at this brochure copy from Paris furniture manufacturer Roche Bobois...

With 235 stores implanted worldwide, Roche Bobois, the noted Paris-based home decor brand, is today a global leader of high-end furniture. The most luxurious materials and leathers, an unsurpassed level of creativity in fabrics all come to life through designer and craftsmen.

Roche Bobois is at the forefront of innovation, especially when it comes to eco-conception. Being responsible for the sustainability of our planet has become n essential element of today's code of good manners. We are committed to developing our products responsibly and to being respectful of the environment.

Welcome to this new issue of the Roche Bobois brochure. Throughout our three collections, Les Contemporains, Les Voyages and Les Pro-vinciales, you will discover some of our latest products and read about current trends in interior design. We offer an extensive choice of dimensions, colors, finishes and materials to answer your vision of the perfect home.

With complementary access to our interior designers, you can let your imagination roam freely and focus on designing a home that is unlike any other but just like you.

See what they have done? In a few short sentences, they have not only established a brand personality, they've managed to:

- convey a general upscale positioning
- brag about the quality and craftsmanship of their furniture
- convey their devotion to personalized service
- set up the education component (UBP) of the brochure...

And all while establishing their company (and culture) as eco-friendly and eco-responsible. You walk away with the impression that not only do they make cool furniture, they care about all citizens of the world and the environment, too.

The three owners of Bludot.com takes their mission of sourcing fun and innovative but affordable design seriously, but not too seriously. The website presents the brand personality, summed up with minimalist simplicity in the website's Bludot Story:

OUR GOAL IS TO BRING GOOD DESIGN TO AS MANY PEOPLE AS POSSIBLE

The three of us were college friends and shared a passion for art, architecture, and design. After we left college and began to furnish our first homes, we didn't like the stuff we could afford and we couldn't afford the stuff we liked. We figured we were not alone and we were naïve enough to try and do something about it. Blu Dot was born in 1997.

Our goal is to bring good design to as many people as possible. Which means creating products that are useful, affordable, and desirable. To make that happen, our design process is founded on collaboration. Not just among ourselves as we play show-and-tell with concepts, but a total collaboration between pencil and paper, materials and machines, even packaging and assembly. We like to think that the form is almost inevitable, a by-product of the process. Our job is simply to help it emerge as beautifully and as efficiently as possible.

Here's what a brand icon remodel for an upscale home remodeling brand...

Founded in 1987 by Patrick and Michael Cunningham, C&C Partners has been recognized by the National Association of Home Builders and *Custom Home* magazine as one of the top custom home-builders in the United States. But the company's original logo projected an outdated 80s feel that was not compelling to the younger, upscale market they were trying to reach.

HOW Creative's new brand icon design overlaid a classic and elegant initial C against a bold and contemporary initial C in elegant colors to reflect the tastes and aspirations of C&C's target market, as well as the contrasting personalities of the two founders. It conveys a brand message of modern but grounded. This is a classic example of inside-out brand design: Brand culture is synchronized with the target customer.

The bottom line is C&C doubled sales, from sales of $3 million to $6 million, and 80 percent of all new business is a direct result of C&C's new brand identity. Authentic brand design helped C&C increase brand value and equity, increase market share, and capture a broader audience.

BEFORE

FRAMED OPENINGS
WINDOWS·DOORS

AFTER

For this wholesaler/retailer of high-end residential doors, windows, skylights and related accessories, HOW Creative's goal was to transform a brand image of neighborhood resource to top-tier, full-service suppliers. Framed Openings' traffic, sales and profits were at a standstill and the brand culture suffered: company morale sagged.

The mission was to create an engaging brand experience for all stakeholders, across all touchpoints. The original logo had a dated "homemade" feel that was incapable of capturing attention outside the neighborhood. The store's business model was skewed to selling on price rather than value.

The store's brand values and identity were reshaped. A revitalized brand image was calibrated to match the quality and sophistication of Framed Openings' products.

A new company brochure — simple, sophisticated and of superior quality — became a key rebranding element.

The company Website matched the brochure's revitalized brand personality. Technological innovation included the addition of e-commerce capability and intuitive navigation design — only two-clicks deep — to ensure fast navigation and simplified selection.

The bottom line of this rebrand? Framed Openings doubled revenues in the first year of the campaign, and quickly expanded. Increases in brand equity and brand value followed, as did increases in market share, customer loyalty and trust. And something else, too: investor interest. A handsome buy offer was made and accepted.

Personality spins out into your brand's universe, consuming — and aligning — the other key elements of the brand. Some successful brands are almost entirely personality — larger-than life personalities. Their symbolic dimension overshadows their physical and functional dimensions. McDonald's is such a brand. The Ronald McDonald personality is the brand.

Other successful brands, like Google, are infused with personality, but personality ultimately takes a back seat to features, quality and performance. The Google personality may have originally attracted you, but the quality of the search experience keeps you. You may love Google's personable holiday graphics, (the shamrock and leprechaun on St. Patrick's day or Santa Claus' cap on Christmas), but you keep coming back because you believe Google offers the most relevant results.

The brand name Google itself conveys a sense of fun — a fun and innovative culture and personality — while managing to suggest the vast universe of mathematical infinity. Google is a fabricated mimetic name, an imitatitve representation or formed word that mimics or imitates another word. Google borrows from the word googol, a term that was coined by a 9-year-old mathematician's son. The definition of *googol* is "the number 10 raised to the power 100 (10 100), written out as the numeral 1 followed by 100 zeros."

The friendly and exuberant animated TiVo character is another example of a personality that takes a back seat to innovation, features and performance. He (she?) hops from screen to screen, accompanying you through the installation and setup experience, but TiVo knows it is features and performance that matters.

The TiVo click sound even has a distinct personality, a brand experience cue that you come to expect, much like AOL's human voice announcing You've Got Mail, which was so entrenched in pop culture that it became the title of a popular Hollywood movie starring Meg Ryan and Tom Hanks.

Often, the very nature of a product — and the general characteristics of the market it is targeting — will color a brand's personality from the get-go. Sometimes personality is inherent in the first inklings of the brand (e.g., a toy company is destined to create a personality that will appeal to kids). But sometimes, as with humans, personality traits do not emerge until later. Remarkable personalities can bubble up during the strategic planning process. The words you use to talk about your brand will begin to attach personality traits.

Never underestimate the power of a likable personality. If you can not be likable, be compelling.

But don not try to create a personalty that appeals to everybody. Appealing to everybody is almost certain to appeal to nobody. Distinctive brand personalities are the ones that succeed out there in the fiercely competitive world of brands. When shaping your personality, it is more important to focus primarily on your unique traits; in other words, the traits that no one else in your category has.

Modify an entire brand category's personality, if you need to. Beer brands, for example, have increased female beer consumption by making beer seem less masculine. Building products brands often appeal to the do-it-yourself market, suggesting that you don't have to be a pro to use their products successfully — anyone can do it. Software developers use this gambit, as well.

One thing to always remember about brand personality is that it shines through whether you intend for it to or not. As with human personality! So intend it. Control it. Hone it. Project a unique personality on purpose.

One final caveat: If you do not give your brand a personality, customers will give you one: Wallflower. And they will walk right by without stopping to engage in conversation.

> **STRATEGY SESSION:**

Imagine that your brand is a person and answer these questions.

EXERCISE:

1. First, work out core demographic and psychographics.

   A. Is your brand female, male, unisex or neither?

   B. Is your brand upscale or value-priced?

   C. Is your brand young, middle age, elderly, ageless?

   D. Is your brand frugal or extravagant?

   E. Is your brand white-collar or blue-collar?

   F. Where does your brand shop for clothes? Home furnishings?

   G. What music does your brand enjoy?

   H. What are your brand's favorite colors?

   I. Is your brand local, regional, national or international?

   J. Is your brand introverted or extroverted?

   K. Is your brand formal or casual?

   L. Is your brand dignified or self-deprecating?

   M. Is your brand the latest thing or the brand with reliable history and experience?

   N. Is your brand urban, suburban exurban or rural?

   O. Is your brand about fast and efficient or slow and seasoned aging?

2. From the list below, choose five unique traits that personify your brand's essence. These should be traits that your costumers can bond with and embrace. For each trait you choose, ask yourself the following questions:

   A. Will these traits differentiate your brand from its competitors?

   B. Can these traits be expressed across all your touchpoints?

   C. Will these traits aim squarely for your target customer mind, heart and gut?

   D. Do these traits realistically portray your product/service and corporate culture?

   E. Will these traits engage an overall memorable brand experience?

PERSONALITY TRAITS

- Witty
- Confident
- Irrational
- Spontanous
- Humorous
- Sassy
- Shy
- Warm
- Honest
- All work, no play
- Light hearted
- Nerdy
- Spiritual
- Creative
- Innocent
- Wise
- Provocative
- Proactive
- Dynamic
- Serious
- Funny
- Demanding
- Soft spoken
- Aggressive
- Cynical
- Loud
- Rational

- Joyous
- Assertive
- Cutting edge
- Humble
- Dynamic
- Simple
- Complex
- Pragmatic
- Educational
- Innovative
- Leadership
- Intelligent
- Fun
- Sexy

(6)

The Brand Experience

The first thing to understand about brand experience is that consumers buy what they *want*, not (necessarily) what they *need*. Once we have what we need, everything after that is a want. And we always want more. We aspire to keep up with the Jones's. We aspire to keep up with our own self-image. And we will spend money to do it.

Sometimes the facts are irrelevant or at least less relevant. The senses take over, ignoring the frontal lobe's rational thoughts, such as:

But this one is more expensive...should it be?

But this one costs more than you can afford!

But this one doesn't have that safety feature...

And the senses reply: I don't care, I want this one!

We will even lie to ourselves to justify buying what we want. We write our own story in our head, creatively editing our own autobiographies...

This Ferrari will change my life forever.

This Rolex will make people respect me.

It happens to the best of us. Why? You ask. Because the one we want is the one that offers the most compelling overall brand experience. We want the one we fall in love with. And the one we fall in love with must live up to our expectations, or we fall out of love just as quickly as we fell in. At the first sign of inconsistency we get nervous, our emotional bond with the brand becomes tenuous. We start looking around for another brand to fall love with.

Branding is fragile because it is perception-based and experience-based. Consumer attitudes can quickly shift to your brand's benefit or detriment. Even stable, megabrands can go into a perceptual skid. Remember Coca Cola's disastrous New Coke vs. Classic Coke branding change in 1985? Ultimately, they actually had to "take it back," reverse a major brand change initiative and pretend that it was just an experiment. It wasn't. It was a major brand revitalization that failed.

Classic Coke is alive and kicking — the product had such brand loyalty that Coca Cola was able to preserve the brand. But you won't find New Coke on the shelves anywhere. In fact, one could argue that it was brand loyalty that triggered the backlash over New Coke. Coke lovers were upset by the thought that their beloved Classic might be replaced.

TOUCHPOINTS ARE THE EXPERIENCE

Your touchpoints will become the visual, auditory and verbal expression of your brand identity, including your brand personality. Touchpoints support, communicate, synthesize and serve as contact points for the brand. Your touchpoints may expand, over time, to a vast matrix of connections with the customer, each reinforcing the last one, creating an expectation for the next one.

Authentic touchpoints burn in customer brand memory — they're the stuff of instant recall and brand memorability. They reinforce your message and identity again and again. They build brand equity. They support your sales efforts, making it faster and easier to close sales.

Authentic brand experience connects the senses, gets them all on the same page.

Your brand's exposure to customers through each touchpoint will either be an asset or a liability. (There is a difference between touchpoints and *authentic touchpoints!*) If any of your touchpoints sends out weak, false, or distorted signals, your brand identity is not integrated, your brand message is open to misinterpretation, and your core values are called into question. You are not inspiring trust — that all-important thread in the fabric of the customer relationship.

Often you find brands whose websites do not match the brochures. There is a disconnect between each medium's use of colors, fonts, copy tonality. The personality of the website and other promotional media does not match the tone of the brand culture you encounter when you actually talk to company employees. The logo on the sign of the company vans does not match the logo on the billboards or the website or the trade show kiosks.

Your touchpoints must be integrated into a single, consistent, credible story; in other words, an *authentic* story.

Your touchpoints might include:

- Brand Icon
- Product, Service, and Company Naming
- Tagline
- Brand Identity Letterhead Systems
- Brochures
- Hand-Outs
- Voicemail
- Direct Mail
- Greeter
- Speeches
- Presentations
- Advertising: Print, electronic, broadcast and outdoor
- Graphic Standard Manuals
- Product Design
- Packaging
- Point of Purchase Displays

- Website
- E-Commerce Solutions
- Web Animation
- 3D Model
- 3D Animation
- Graphic User Interface
- Trade Show Booth Design
- Illustration
- Kiosk Design
- Character Design
- Signage
- Vehicle Signage
- Motion Graphics / On Air
- Book Cover Designs
- Posters
- Merchandising
- Special Promotion Materials
- Presentation Folders
- Binder Design
- Catalog Sheets

If you plan to develop even a few of these, you can see why it will be critical to develop an integrated touchpoint plan, instead of pitching your touchpoints out there, fingers crossed, hoping that one of them will gain stickiness in the consumer's mind. Each of them must stick. Stickiness is a cumulative state; it occurs over time, and is the result of careful brand execution and management.

BRANDING FOR THE SENSES

An authentic brand experience is a sensory experience.

Ninety percent of our sensory experiences are visual. But authentic brand experiences utilize every possible sensory modality. Color, shape, size, sound, scent and touch are all sensory cues which consumers use to identify, categorize and evaluate products. We intuitively decode the language of product attributes using what are often referred to as "implicit product theories."

For example, car manufacturers use scent ("new car smell") and sound (the sound an engine revving or the thud of car door closing) to evoke conscious or subconscious feelings of qualities such as newness, quality, luxury or sportiness. We also devise our own implicit theories based on our personal beliefs; for example: *If I buy a Japanese-made cars, it will be of a higher quality and have better resale value.*

Consumers, in fact, develop beliefs about brand attributes with amazingly little brand-specific information. They thin-slice and evaluate products in seconds, with very little information to go on.

Research has shown that people often use visual information that is not even directly related to the product to form inferences about the product's characteristics. For example, a customer walks into a home furnishings emporium for the first time. The products are distinctive and high-quality, but unfortunately the store is housed in a shabby building in a crumbling warehouse district. The customer may form negative inferences about the products before she's even had an opportunity to inspect them; she's primed to believe that the quality of the store environment will be reflected in the products.

We are deeply influenced by sensory stimulation, whether we are consciously aware of it or not.

If you walk into a movie theatre and smell the familiar and expected aroma of freshly popped popcorn, does it inspire you to buy popcorn? But what happens if you walk into a Wal-Mart and the aroma of stale popcorn is wafting about? Are you inspired to buy popcorn while you shop? Or do you find yourself trying to marginalize or ignore the popcorn aroma, associating it perhaps with a cheap carnival atmosphere where people wandering around munching food while exploring the attractions?

Two physical product attributes — color and shape — add a symbolic dimension to brand perception... and brand personality. People are usually unaware of the powerful impact that color and shape have on their perception of a product, or of a brand. But color and shape can actually accomplish three key tasks:

1. Attract attention

2. Activate emotions and trigger a response

3. Generate perceptive illusions

The physical structure and visual characteristics of a product and its packaging add a psychological load that influences the customer perception of the brand's personality. A product's physical appearance (e.g., color and shape) can add load in feelings of calmness or serenity. Excitement and energy. Innovative and high-tech. Intriguing and mysterious.

Product color, shape and packaging influences customer expectations of a product. For example, it would not be a good idea to market a tranquilizer medication in a red package. Red arouses and excites. Blue or green would obviously be better choices. Red, on the other hand would be a better choice for an energy drink, as opposed to a tranquil seafoam green.

Color influences three aspects of brand personality:

Excitement

Sophistication

Competence

The color of a web page's background can even influence the perception of how fast the page is downloading. The feeling of relaxation that blue evokes can create the perception of faster downloading; i.e., competence. Studies have shown that more positive retail outcomes occur in blue rather than red environments. Blue retail environments apparently stimulate an inclination to shop and browse. Surprised? These results suggest that the overall affective sensory perception of a color may actually be more powerful than the arousal aspect of color.

Color is a differentiating element that can be especially powerful for products whose technical characteristics are standardized, boring or trivial. Color can be used not only to draw attention to a product, but to strengthen the visual identity of the brand, as well. And we process that color identity almost instantaneously.

Tachistoscope studies reveal interesting facts about human perception of color. A tachistoscope, in case you're curious, is a device that projects images onto a screen at rapid speed; it's often used to test visual perception, memory, and learning. Anyway, when subjects were shown certain colors for a fraction of a second and asked to indicate the first color they perceived, the results showed:

Orange	21.4%
Red	18.6%
Blue	17.0%
Yellow	12.0%

Color can create perceptive illusions; for example, blue areas look smaller than yellow areas. Color can modify a customer's perception of the size and the weight of an object. Red and yellow objects tend to be overestimated; blue and green objects tend to be more accurately estimated.

Shape, like color, helps customers categorize and differentiate products. We have built-in shape biases for many brand categories. Sometimes it is because the shape chosen by the brand leader has pre-conditioned us to believe that this is the proper shape and any other shape is "wrong." Visualize the shapes of a Heinz Ketchup bottle and a Coca-Cola bottle… Can you imagine Heinz Ketchup packaged in a Coke bottle? Or Coke packaged in a Heinz Ketchup bottle? Can you imagine elegant ladies perfume packaged in a tin can?

But "unexpected" shapes can also be powerful attention-grabbers. For Phillips Media's Burn Cycle media game, HOW Creative designed a dynamic triangular package with arresting, shock-color graphics to halt eye-scan and grab buyer attention.

Shape can influence the perceived volume or weight of a product, which can impact a consumer's attitude about the product's value. Shape can create perceptive illusions. Human developmental research has long shown that containers that are tall and thin often appear to "hold more" than containers that are short and fat.

Shapes are also associated with psychological meanings. For example, a few studies shown that people associate sweetness with roundness. Bitterness with non-round shapes — especially triangular shapes.

As you build your brand, bear in mind that sensory stimulation can dramatically impact the customer's brand experience and ultimately influence behavior. For example, HOW Creative designed sassy, interactive packaging for Sassy Stables, Funrise Products' line of toys for young girls. A voice chip allows animatronic horses to speak to customers, and with plenty of attitude.

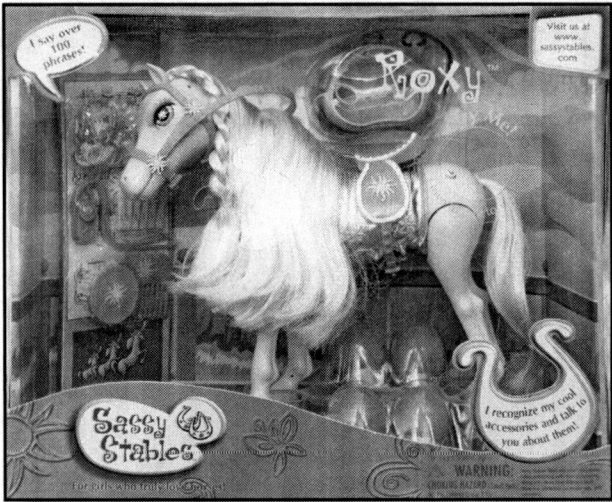

BUILDING A PERSUASIVE BRAND

In the new economy, marketers are redefining their persuasion systems to forge stronger emotional connections. Profits and brand equity depend on persuasion.

Here is the cold truth: Most people won't buy your product. Either they can't afford it, don't want it, or don't have time to listen to your pitch. You can't sell them if they ignore your pitch, and you can't sell them if they do listen to your pitch, but aren't persuaded. And many prospects who would conceivably buy your product may never even hear about it.

First you must persuade people to pay attention to you…to your brand icon, your message, your product. Then you must persuade them to buy your product.

The best way to convince someone to do something they do not want to do is to get them to want to do it. Easier said than done, right? Not if you know which levers to pull.

ELIMINATE THE RISK FACTOR

While we are always on the lookout for new products to get excited about, we have a built-in purchase resistance to an unknown brand. If you are the new kid on the block, you've got some persuading to do. If you are a little guy battling a behemoth of a brand leader, you have got some persuading to do.

Closing the sale means removing the obstacles from the buying decision; in other words — winning a customer's trust. Making it easier, faster, richer, deeper, cooler, more fun, superior…risk-free.

People usually buy the product they think they should have. To understand this behavioral insecurity, you need to understand how risk is perceived. There are essentially five kinds of risk in every buying decision:

- **Monetary** (Will I lose money?)
- **Functional** (What if it doesn't work?)
- **Physical** (Can this thing hurt me?)
- **Social (**Will my peers approve?)
- **Psychological** (Will this make me feel guilty or irresponsible?)

You must create the perception that your product does not carry these risks. If you are really lucky (or really clever), your differentiating attribute can eliminate several risks in one blow. Being the market leader, for example, eliminates most of them. People love adventurous new products, but tend to buy them from whomever they perceive to be the leader. (If everyone else thinks this is the best product, it must be.)

Once the market's collective mind is made up, it is virtually impossible to change it. Consider, for example, how many artificial sweeteners

have fallen from grace over the years. Once you're out, you're out —
particularly if there was a risk factor attached to your product's fall
from grace. (For example, it was recently discovered to cause cancer in
rats. Tough to redeem a brand in a predicament like this.)

In general, people fall into four buyer personality types in terms of how
they evaluate information, assess risk, and make decisions:

1. Intuitives
2. Thinkers
3. Feelers
4. Sensors

Intuitives focus on possibilities, and tend to avoid details. They're big-pic-
ture types who love the idea of the "next generation" product. The
intuitive prefers to absorb information in an abstract form, as ideas, images, or concepts. From the initial concept, they'll develop a conceptual
framework or structure, into which they can fit the details later.

Thinkers like precision, logic and analytical thinking. They're good at
processing details, and are less likely to let emotion "get in the way."
Technical details — specifics — appeal to this crowd. The thinker
makes decisions based on facts, data, details. They ask questions such
as: *What will it cost me? Can I afford it? Will I be sorry tomorrow?*

Feelers make decisions based on feelings, emotions, personal values,
and interpersonal relationships. They ask questions such as: *How am I
going to feel driving this new car?* They're always susceptible to the feelings
of others. They shun intellectual analysis and bend to their personal
likes and dislikes. Once they like you, they tend to be loyal customers.
They make for good testimonials because their endorsements have an
authentic personal style.

Sensors respect concrete facts and have an exceptionally good eye for
detail. They prefer details first, building an understanding of the overall concept through the details, step by step. And they prefer to learn
through the senses — touch, sight, sound, taste and smell. They like to

pick things up, turn them over, see all sides. Theyre adept at establishing context, and perceiving things are they really are. They're rarely wrong.

One of these four buyer personalities is almost always dominating any given purchase decision. Certainly, buyers may display characteristics of more than one personality type on any given day. But we tend to be more comfortable working, learning and functioning as one "type" more than the others.

Make sure your touchpoints accommodate the buyer personality that most closely aligns with your customer's psychographics. That's part of the journey to authenticity.

BUILD BY THESE BRAND PERSUASION PRINCIPLES

As you build your brand, never lose sight of these Brand Persuasion Principles. They are critical to building a persuasive system for the new economy:

Brand Affinity. (Apple) People do business with people — and companies — they like. We're more likely to invest in someone with whom we empathize and feel affinity. We choose brands that seem most like us, brands whose personalities align with our own, brands whose image aligns with our own self-image. Personality is your most important ally in your battle to build affinity.

Brand Leadership. (BMW) People tend to rely on the brand they perceive to be the leading brand, the authoritative brand. They assume that the leading brand must be doing something right, after all — that there's a reason why they're the leader.

Brand Consistency. (Bayer Aspirin) We value consistency in other people, and in the products and services we buy. The surest way to kill a brand is to launch it, build affinity for it in the marketplace, then change it. (You've heard the old adage about the dangers of changing horses mid-stream.) Don't offer features and benefits then eliminate them. Or make brand statements then contradict them.

Brand Consensus. (Epinions.com or Consumer Report) In any social situation, people tend to observe what other people do in order to decide how to act. Often consensus is built on tiny, seemingly unimportant aspects of a product, eventually leading to the tipping point. Never before has Brand Consensus been more persuasive than it is in the new internet economy. Product reviews and recall announcements, for example, can ripple across the blogosphere in nanoseconds.

Brand Reciprocity. (Salvation Army) People feel obligated to return a favor. Someone makes a concession, hoping for, in return, a concession by the other party. It's the age-old concept of "tit for tat" or "stick and carrot," and it's the heart and soul of negotiation. And make no mistake, every purchase decision is a negotiation, even if only in the mind of the prospect. Giving a customer something free of charge is one good way to inspire reciprocity. There's one catch, though: the customer must perceive the item to have value.

Now, there's a sixth persuasion principle that can be powerful in certain market niches (e.g., the prestige market):

Scarcity. (Aston Martin) This is the old First Come, First Served retail trick of creating the perception of "limited quantity." People value what they believe to be scarce or rare.

⑦

Telling an Authentic Story

Every brand is a story. That story must be authentic if the brand is to succeed in the short term and be sustainable over the long term.

The story you tell is ongoing. It unfolds over time, bit by bit, with each new touchpoint a customer encounters. That is the power of authentic branding: It lets brands create meaningful dialogues over time, cultivating and deepening customer relationships with each touchpoint encounter, guiding them down the path from awareness to engagement, to purchase, and ultimately to loyalty.

Consumers trust good storytellers, and trust, of course, is required for that emotional connection.

Let us look at some elements of authentic brand stories...

An authentic story is *true*. Your story must be factually true. Truth has become a rare quality in today's marketplace — practically a collectible. Consumers are thrilled and inspired by stories that turn out to be true; in other words, brands that meet or exceed their expectations.

If you tell customers they can trust your brand because all your products are made from all-natural ingredients, they had better be made from all-natural ingredients. If you tell customers that your products are safe kids, they had better be safe for kids. If you tell customers that your restaurant serves only fresh, home-cooked food, you better not get caught serving store-bought frozen food.

Consider Enron's fall from grace... They painted a fraudulent portrait of the company's financial health and raided the employees' pension fund. Once the accounting scandals were uncovered, Enron was a goner. Nothing they could say would ever restore public trust. If you get caught lying — whether it is in an ad or a speech made by your CEO — your brand is a liar, you have betrayed the customer, and odds are good that nothing you say after that will reinstate trust.

An authentic story is consistent. Your story must not contradict itself over the course of your brand's life. Just look what happens to politicians who "flip-flop." Remember John Kerry's disastrous "I actually did vote for the $87 billion before I voted against it" snafu in the 2004 presidential election? His political enemies truncated his explanation to "I was for it before I was against it" (code for: *This candidate is inauthentic*) and repeated it again and again.

Kerry had previously implied that voting against wartime funding bills was equivalent to abandoning the troops. Then a year after voting to support the use of force in Iraq, Kerry voted against an $87 billion supplemental funding bill for U.S. troops in Iraq and Afghanistan. It did not seem to matter much that he opposed the bill because it contained Bush administration tax cuts, or that he did support an alternative bill that funded the $87 billion by cutting some of those tax cuts. It was more than — as he described it — "an inarticulate moment." It was viewed by many as an inauthentic moment, and a ding to his credibility. Carefully nuanced positions are mistrusted. They smell inauthentic.

Each touchpoint is an element of your story, and you never know which touchpoint a customer will encounter. If your story is consistent across all your touchpoints, you help the customer fashion each element into a coherent and believable story. That is an authentic story.

An authentic brand uses a consistent voice across all touchpoints — from the website and brochure copy to point-of-sale displays and billboards. Familiarity breeds camaraderie, affinity, trust and loyalty.

An authentic story makes a promise. It may promise fun, excitement, safety, financial savings, time savings, efficiency, speed or [substitute your brand promise here]. The promise should be bold, exceptional, and different from the promises your competitors make. Consider the earnest promise Avis made to differentiate the Avis brand from category leader, Hertz: *We try harder.*

And, of course, the promise must be kept. Customers noticed that Avis tried harder, and Avis became the category leader. They kept using the tagline. It was a value proposition that they actually honored, and a badge of authenticity.

An authentic story engages customers quickly. First impressions — thin slices — can be immensely powerful. Customers become engaged the second the story clicks into place. But it must click into place quickly.

Today's consumers are far too impatient to sort every fact presented to them, and they will thin-slice your product whether you want them to or not. First, they concoct a quick theory about the brand, then they look for evidence to support their theory. In other words, they are already telling themselves a story, and they will do everything they can to prove that their initial judgment was correct.

You may not have time, in your first impression, to appeal to logic. But you always have time to appeal to the senses. One whiff of a perfume, one glimpse of a sexy car can engage — and even intoxicates. After all, when we meet a new person for the first time, we tend to decide on the spot whether we like them or not, in the first few seconds of the encounter.

No customer will continue to listen to your story until you have earned the credibility to tell it.

An authentic story does not obfuscate, confuse or trick people. When evaluating products or services, consumers grasp for easy-to-process, unambiguous information that has direct and obvious implications for them. Communicate succinctly how your brand will make their life better. Be careful about using too much technical jargon or confusing terminology, especially when presenting products or services to the mainstream.

Many companies with vast product lines feel compelled to show off. But tossing large and confusing product assortments at a customer does not lead to greater interest. It only strengthens the customer's desire for cognitive closure — definite, concrete knowledge. Researchers have also found that this human need for cognitive closure is so strong that it will cause most consumers to "freeze" their initial judgments and refrain from considering additional evidence that could potentially threaten that closure. Once we find closure, we do not like to upset the apple cart.

Never try to confuse customers about exactly what they're getting and how much they're paying for it. They shouldn't have to read the fine print to figure out how much it's *really* going to cost them. Long-distance calling plans and credit card promotions are notorious offenders. Some of them are so confusing that their own customer service reps don't understand them.

An authentic story contains believable characters and plots. The greatest literary works are free of contrived characters and plots. So are the best brand stories. Does the image of that gorgeous, statuesque blonde "housewife" scrubbing her kid's "hard-to-clean" gunk off the floor with some miraculous new floor cleaner ring true? We haven't been able to get by with that stuff since the 1960s. (Remember Leave It To Beaver's June Cleaver vacuuming the living room in a dress, high heels and pearls?)

False notes make customers suspicious. Or get you laughed at. Neither is an auspicious start down the path to authenticity.

A character does not have to be human to be authentic. The Pillsbury Doughboy, animated M&Ms... they are authentic and believable, even though we know they are not real. M&Ms do not dance. They lie perfectly still in their little wrapper. When you open a Pillsbury cannister, no dough boy pops out, giggling.

What all these inhuman creations have is *humanity*. Their creators breathed life into them, endowing them with sheer force of personality and an ability to tell you things about the product that no brochure or fact sheet ever could.

By contrast, consider the fast food hamburger category's bizarre Jack in the Box spokescharacter...Jack, presumably? Certainly he is a differentiated character, but do you find him engaging and likable? Or trustable? Or believable? And he is an actual human, albeit one wearing an androgynous, ambiguous, geometric toy-head.

An authentic story lets customers draw their own conclusions. Sometimes the less a marketer spells out, the more powerful the story becomes. Realize that even as you are telling an authentic story, the customer may be telling themselves a lie, building some complicated, involved tale that justifies how this new purchase will fulfill her deepest needs (which are probably, in truth, wants). Customers fill in those blanks with their feelings. You can not do that for them.

Good and authentic stories let us lie to ourselves. And those lies satisfy our desires. In a sense, it is the story, not the product or service you sell, that pleases the customer.

Think about the story you are already telling yourself when you answer the phone and it is a telemarketer, who promptly launches into the long, pre-scripted spiel you were dreading, not even stopping to draw a breath until eight sentences later. No one wants to hear an inauthentic telemarketer's story. The story was not written for you. It was written for whoever that phone number happens to belong to. It is marketing to the masses, not marketing to one.

An authentic story matches the customer's worldview. The most believable stories are the ones we already agreed with, whether we knew it or not. Your touchpoints should reinforce the beliefs of your target market. The more skilled you are at aiming squarely for your target with each of your communications (e.g., targeted commercial time slots), the more likely you are to hit the target.

An authentic story is not for everyone. It is for *you*.

8

The Design Revolution:
Innovating & Differentiating Through Authentic Brand Design

Authentic brand design is much bigger than product design or graphic design. Sure, product design and graphic design is part of the larger synchronicity, but it is not the sum of a brand's authenticity. Authentic brand design aligns the organization's product design and graphic design with its core brand values. Every design element — from the brand icon to the product packaging — is inextricably tied to the core philosophy of the brand. The result is a brand that is sustainable over time, and continues to accumulate equity and long-term value.

The long and checkered history of the Ford Mustang is a perfect example of what happens when a once-authentic brand design slips into inauthenticity. When Ford launched the first Mustang in 1964, a buying frenzy ensued. Exuberant consumers descended on Ford showrooms, vying to be the first to own a Mustang. Legend has it that those buyers even slept in their chosen cars overnight, while waiting for their checks to be approved.

But throughout the eight generations of '70s, '80s and early '90s Mustang IIs and Cobras, the authenticity of the Mustang brand began to unravel. Ford dramatically decreased the Mustang's raw horsepower to comply with the fuel efficiency standards of the day, and followed the rounded-edge car design trends, instead of leading the design trend. The Mustang lost its spirit, its muscle, and its identity. As the years passed, it looked more and more generic, a mere shadow of its former self. By the way, what is a "Mustang Cobra" anyway? Some unnatural horse-reptile hybrid? The Mustang brand no longer stood for anything in the marketplace, thus sales reflected that.

Ford, to their credit, understood that killing the Mustang would kill the one car that the whole world associated with Ford. The Mustang's brand identity had fused with Ford's core identity. With the 2005 redesign, they returned to their brand roots.

They gave their core market the brand they craved. The resurrected the original, classic American muscle car… the throaty rumble, the classic Mustang sharp-edged design with its canted nose, big grille and round headlights reminiscent of the '67 to '69 Mustangs, while the side sculpting, fastback roofline and taillights recall the '65 ponies. It does not even look like the other modern muscle cars. It looks like a Mustang, and the American love affair with the Mustang was reborn.

It is a cautionary tale. Authentic brand designs such as Porsche, Aston Martin, Bentley have remained consistent and sustained brand value. It is clear who they are and who they are does not change.

HOW IMPORTANT IS DESIGN?

Design visionaries can completely revolutionize corporate cultures and business strategies. And visionary design — product design and graphic design — can completely revolutionize a customer's opinion of your brand.

Customers are inspired by great brand experiences, and those experiences can be framed by design. Sensory-driven design moves us, stimulates us, inspires and delights us. Great design can transform a ho-hum brand encounter into an emotional brand experience. Great design is a language all its own, the ultimate evocative and provocative expression of a brand.

What can great design do for you? It differentiates your brand from the other boring stuff in the marketplace. It lifts your products and company out of sameness and similarity. It elevates you above the brandscape monotony that gives customers an excuse to tune out, and provides them with a reason to tune in.

Design, for many brands, reflects the core brand identity — is the core brand identity. Take Nike. Let's say you wanted to buy the Nike brand and Nike was willing to sell it. Nike quotes a price, and it sounds good to you. Then they tell you that price buys everything — inventory, manufacturing facilities, accounts receivable, everything — *except* the Nike brand swoosh mark and the name *Nike.*

Bet you'd change your mind now, wouldn't you? In terms of future brand sustainability in the marketplace, you would not get much value for your money!

See the power of authentic brand design? The Nike trade name is more than a word. It is a lifestyle. The Nike brand mark is more than a simple, swooshy brushstroke. It is a collection of intangible assets — implied meanings, subtextual messages and emotional associations in the minds of consumers. Those intangibles form the very essence of Nike. It is where Nike is heading and what Nike will become. It is Nike's core brand identity and its brand image. The core values, identity *and* image are aligned.

Consider the tech industry and electronics market, where design and engineering can make or break a product. As technological break-throughs happen, design and engineering must innovate to keep up, and ideally work together to advance the brand. In brand categories where a product's design features are the reason to buy or not buy, design is the brand.

Sometimes a product's design implementation — the execution — can be not only a differentiating factor and huge usability factor, but a brand-building, category-building factor as well. Apple set a new technology standard with the original iPod's versatile but minimal-ist thumbwheel, then did it again with the iPhone and iPod touch's elegant and responsive multisensory touchscreen. The iPhone, in fact, launched a whole new category of smartphones and the other smart-phones suddenly looked a whole lot dumber.

All fashion brands depend on innovative design to sell product. The product is not a product without great design. All successful fashion brands must reinvent themselves over and over again, while retaining the brand's core essence. A brand is only as good as next season's line. Apparel brands like Dolce & Gabbana and Armani survive and thrive on distinctive tailoring and in vogue design.

Entire brands can be built around design. Authentic, original design can build authentic brands.

Consider the category of bicycle manufacturers whose bicycles are priced in the mid- to low-price point ranges (e.g., Huffy) and sold through big-box retailers such as Toys 'R Us, Target, K-Mart, Wal-Mart and sporting goods stores. Their high-end bike models may include special performance and durability features such as more shifting speeds, solid steel frames, special mountain terrain tires, or a pro racer seat. But because they are sold at lower prices points, the caliber of these features is not intended to compete with that of a bike shop bike such as Trek, Fuji or Gary Fisher.

By and large, cosmetic design sells a Huffy bike: the bicycle's frame design, graphical decals, paint finish, and accessories. The bulk of the design burden is borne by the paint finish and the graphics on the decal. A cool metallic paint finish and a cool typeface with cool special effects can sell the bike.

Design has dramatically changed the brandscape. It adds a whole new layer of messenging that is usually less expensive to execute, and lasts beyond your most recent commercial. It is, in a sense, its own advertising. In fact, if the product is recalled more readily than the commercial, you know you have got a winning brand. Design is a message that customers take home with them, in the packaging or in the product itself — ideally both.

Great design, in many successful, authentic brands, is the brand experience. Great design is relevant design. Design should have purpose and express an emotional reality.

Great design generates buzz. It breathes life into ideas. It can flaunt itself just by existing. It brags about the brand so that you do not have to.

People "get it" without explanation. And it fosters a corporate culture of innovation that builds sustainable brands.

THE FEMINIZING OF DESIGN

Female consumers are leading design trends and message development. In fact, roughly 80 percent of today's buying decisions are influenced by women. Design, like all other elements of branding, must make an emotional connection.

Emotional design is usually design + style. That does not meant that men are being forced to buy "girly" products. It means that design must be driven by the emotional aspects of lifestyle, culture, and aspiration. Too many designers are still caught in a time warp; they fear that designing to appeal to women means that you must color everything pink. It doesn't. But what it does mean is that you must seek to forge an emotional connection that would persuade women to buy.

More women are living alone these days, which requires them to be more deeply involved in all aspects of household purchases. They are not just buying appliances, window treatments, and cleaning products anymore, or the occasional can of wall paint. They are buying plywood and gypsum board and hammers and nails and drill drivers and nail guns. They are looking for independence and control. And enterprising product designers are designing products and promotional materials to accommodate them, both aesthetically and functionally.

The smartest designers know how to filter outside research, input from other strategists, and environmental stimuli and arrive at their own unique design interpretations. Their emotional connections to culture, art and people are have become much more than a casual or complementary research approach. Research, in the new economy, should be driven by inspired ideas, as opposed to letting ideas be driven by research. Designers must seek fresh, innovative ways to elicit emotional responses from design.

Such design innovation is emerging everywhere, in even the most mundane of products.

In 2006, Mazola modernized both its brand identity and the 47-year-old pan-spray market with the debut of a healthier, alcohol-free Mazola Pure oil. Instead of encasing Mazola Pure in the usual steel cylinder, the company designed a curvy plastic container with an appealing iridescent finish that looks more like a deodorant bottle or feminine hair spray bottle than a cooking spray can. The result? Mazola Pure overtook established brands to become the number two cooking spray.

Makita is known for engineering and design innovations that make power tools lighter, more efficient and "feel better to use." Using a tagline of Feel/Innovation and an extended brand name of "Makita Industrial Power Tools," Makita's recent messaging promotes qualities that have traditionally been viewed as feminine, while retaining the necessary masculine attributes of power and professional craftsmanship. They are building a brand essence around the concept of *Feel*:

> When your tools Feel better, you Feel better. And when you Feel better, a job isn't just a job, it's an opportunity to demonstrate how powerful you can be. And when the job is done, you'll still have energy to do the things you love.

VISUAL ASSETS ARE FINANCIAL ASSETS

Your visual assets — from your brand icon and logo to your packaging — can turn a commodity product into a premium product, a product that becomes a valuable financial asset. The brand identity is owned by the company, but the brand image is owned by customers. Wrapped up in that brand image is their expectation of a product, service and company, which your visual assets can quickly convey across every touchpoint encounter, again and again.

The five tangible assets that are most important to a company's brand are:

1. The mark/brand icon/logo

2. The name

3. Font/typographical look

4. Colors

5. Tagline

Every other visual touchpoint stems from — and repeats — these elements. Each of these five elements should be expressed consistently across all touchpoints. And each of these five elements must be compatible with each other, conveying consistent personality and meaning.

BRAND ICON

The brand icon is the most important, most tangible element of brand identity, and over time, it becomes a symbol of authentic brand design.

The brand icon is a symbol that can be recognized quickly — ideally, instantly, with no pause between cognition and recognition. That symbol becomes immediately and positively associated with your company. The brand icon wraps the essence of your company in a simple, evocatively expressive form. Your brand icon becomes the symbolic representation of your company, conveying who you are (your core brand identity) and what you sell. When you design your brand icon, develop it with the intent to advance your brand. Design a timeless icon that will wear well in the future.

Your Brand Icon should provoke immediate and positive emotion. In time, it should become a visual asset that elevates brand recall and creates instant, positive images about its source. When you see the Red Cross' red cross brand icon, what feelings are evoked? Perhaps that the Red Cross is empathetic, caring, altruistic — helping people in need without expecting anything in return. And the red conveys urgency, like a red STOP sign.

Brand icons make a brand's life easier. When designing a brand icon, your objectives should include:

- Making it easy to build brand equity

- Making it easy for the customer to buy

- Making it easy for the sales force to sell

TYPES OF BRAND MARKS

A brand mark should be quickly recognizable, and immediately provoke emotion. Words must be decoded into meaning — what the brand means to the customer. The mark should be so good that it can stand alone. You should be able to remove it from a logotype or other element and it would still be recognizable.

Types of brand marks include: Word Mark, Pictorial Mark, Abstract Mark, Letterform Mark and Emblem Mark.

Word Mark. A freestanding word or group of words (usually a company name or an acronym) in which readability, impact and uniqueness are key. Word marks are used to convey a brand attribute, or product positioning, or both. Font selection and, frequently, the use of a custom-designed font, are critical to the word mark's power. It is effective when communicating stability, experience and leadership.

Cartoon Network. A mark redesigned to be in 'toon with the times. Retains the original brand essence, while adding more personal elements: icons relevant to young viewers and a pair of winsome, cartoonish eyes.

CLUESTONES™

Cluestones. A unique genealogy service that discovers, reconstructs and preserves a family's history in both narrative and pictorial form. The magnifying glass graphic symbolizes their name, while capturing the investigative nature of their mission.

Pictorial Mark. This symbolic graphic form is a literal, recognizable image that utilizes shapes first, color second, and content third. It may allude to the company's name, or suggest the company's purpose, or be symbolic of a brand's compelling attributes.

LA Marathon. A free-form figure inspired a new spirit for this world-class event. This stylized single runner concept captured the essence of marathon running — speed, stamina and solitary effort.

Stander. A mark that personifies freedom of movement and freedom of choice for a company that distributes devices and equipment that make life easier for senior citizens and others who have impaired mobility. The Stander brand represents client sensitivity, quality merchandise and, ultimately, freedom of movement.

Abstract Mark. A representational graphic form that symbolically communicates a complex or multifaceted message. It's an excellent vehicle to embody the brand's vision and brand attributes. Abstract marks are also especially useful for companies with many diverse outreaches or divisions.

Piano Wizard. Is an innovative educational and entertaining game that teaches people to play the piano. Piano Wizard employs color-coding as a teaching technique. The elliptical image seems to be in motion through the use of a color palette that matches colors used in the game.

Razalin. A warm, fuzzy spiral flower image in soft tones, desert colors subtly captures the flavor of a desert-based chain of greeting cards/ stationary stores.

Letterform Mark. A single letter becomes the brand mark. This letter is made proprietary through custom design that integrates the mark with the brand's personality and meaning. Letterforms are quickly grasped, rich in graphic impact and emotional symbolism.

Individual Suited. This simple and slightly whimsical letterform uses the lower case letter *i* as a representation of an individual customer and his personal style. The i humanizes the company, which sells custom-tailored suits in fine fabrics from around the world for a fraction of the price you'd expect.

Divine Indulgence. Heavenly designs that can make any table, sofa or chair look elegant and sophisticated. The simple yet elegant D and I are integrated as a system — oneness, in keeping with their mission for every assignment.

Emblem Mark. These marks are built around a pictorial element that is incapable of being disentangled, because they are integrated into the company's name. The mark and the name are integrated. Especially effective in product packaging, signage and embroidered emblems.

Gift. GIFT produces inspiring CDs and books specially formatted and structured to facilitate easier reading for people with Attention Deficit Disorder (ADD).

UCSB ACCESS. Innovative UCSB set the stand for nationwide Student ID cards that double as debit cards. A human fingerprint —the finger-print of each card's owner — symbolizes the individuality of both the company, the product and the product's function.

BRAND NAME

Your goal for your brand name is to make it become part of your prospect's vocabulary. You want your brand name to known, respected and trusted by your prospects. You want them to hear the name and associate it with authenticity. Quite a challenge, eh? Maybe. But it is the one element that your brand may have to live with forever.

The competition to create a unique and powerful brand name is fierce. If you have ever done name searches, you probably figured out quickly that most of the good names are taken.

The competition for memorability in the mind of the customer is fierce, too. The human mind can retain perhaps 50,000 words, but there are more than a million trademarks out there in the marketplace vying for attention!

Buyers generally buy brands, not companies. Sure, there are successful companies whose names add credibility to any new brand they launch — Coca Cola, 3M and IBM are notable examples. But even in those cases, that credibility originally emerged from those companies' brand identities.

Brand Name Types:

- Founder (H.H. Gregg & Sons)
- Descriptive (Brawny, Hefty)
- Fabrication (Google)
- Metaphor (Dove, Cougar, Jaguar, Thunderbird)
- Acronym (I.B.M., G.E.)
- Double Entendre (Staples)
- Composition (Sunkist, FedEx, Drano, Windex)

Wherever possible, a brand name should evoke appropriate (and emotional) images, and establish some sort of kinship with the customer, and appeal to their personal taste. The name should *sound* pleasing when spoken. It should send a message that is sharp, precise and clear.

When testing names, test for:

1. **Comprehension.** They "get" your message
2. **Recollection.** They remember the name
3. **Appeal.** The name appeals to them psychologically and they are motivated to investigate

TAGLINES

Authentic, compelling taglines evoke an immediate emotional response. Your tagline advertises an offering truthfully to your market, based on your value innovation.

An authentic tagline should so unique that it can be protected legally.

Rules for Writing an Effective Tagline

Brevity. It must be short.

Separation. It must differentiate your brand from the competition.

Singularity. It must capture the singularity of your product.

Positioning. It must effectively position your product

Memorability. It must be easy-to-remember and powerfully expressed.

Positive. It cannot offer any unintended negative connotations.

Recognizable. It must be quickly recognizable, even at a small point size.

Types of Taglines

Provocative (thought-provoking: frequently a question)

Comparative (positions the company or brand against its competitors; usually as best in class or category leader)

Aspirational (encourages consumers to achieve or improve; often begins with a verb)

Imperative (includes a call to action; often begins with a verb)

Descriptive (defines and clarifies the product, service, company or brand promise)

Let us dissect some successful taglines…

Three beverage brands built their strategies around refreshment and lifestyle choices…

Sprite: *Obey Your Thirst.*

Mountain Dew: *Do the Dew.*

Budweiser: *Where there's life, there's Bud*

For Sprite, thirst quenching drove the tagline. Mountain Dew equated their drink to a cultural movement. Budweiser became the life in "the life of the party." In each instance, the branding was built on separation, creating a solitary niche where the product's unique qualities could best be displayed.

Here is a breakfast food builds a tagline around its identity as an unusual shape:

Cheerios. Smiles all round.

Gerber built its message on the natural nurturing instinct of its target audience, mothers of newborn babies:

Shouldn't your baby be a Gerber baby?

Apple Computer built its Macintosh messaging around the radical differences between the Mac and IBM and IBM-clone PCs, conveying the Mac's unique "thinking" and functional abilities and friendly, intuitive graphical user interface, while taking a swipe at competitor's platforms:

Macintosh: Think different.

Some time later, IBM fought globally:

IBM: Solutions for a small planet

MetLife (Metropolitan Life Insurance) avoided mentioning death, delivering a classy, euphemistically effective message that just happened to also be a pun:

Have you met life today?

American Express became a cultural icon with just a few well-chosen words:

Don't Leave Home Without It

At a time when "banker's hours" actually meant something, one bank started a trend that continues to this day:

Your Citi never sleeps

Toyota's tagline suggested that their alternative energy vehicle's environmental roots did not mean their car was a wuss:

Prius. Mean but green.

The U.S. Post Office had trouble delivering packages overnight. FedEx boldly stepped in and guaranteed overnight delivery. The result? FedEx owns the phrase overnight delivery:

When it absolutely, positively has to get there overnight

Hallmark managed to elevate their quality of their greeting cards above the competition and, in the same breath, flatter the customer and build affinity:

Because you care enough to send the very best

BRAND COLORS

Color builds meaning and instantly conveys brand personality and brand attributes. Your ultimate goal is to own a color that conveys your core brand essence, a color that customers will ultimately come to associate with your brand. Color contributes to brand equity, and color consistency over the long haul can help burn a brand into the customer's mind.

In the soft drink market, Coke owns red. In the courier market, UPS decided to own brown (dependable/reliable) to differentiate itself from FedEx, who already owned innovation and friendliness with purple and orange. (FedEx also chose the two most shocking colors it could find so that its packages would stand out on the recipient's desk.)

Kodak is yellow. Fuji is green.

Hertz is yellow. Avis is red. National is green.

When brands become leaders, the colors they choose come to symbolize or even personify them. We subliminally translate colors to symbols because we associate color with meanings.

Colors have different connotations in different cultures, so it is important to research your target market and determine how your color choices will resonate with them. For example, in the U.S., white symbolizes weddings and purity, but in some Eastern cultures, white symbolizes mourning. In the U.S., black is the color of mourning. But it is also the color of luxury (e.g., Johnnie Walker Black Label). Blue is the color of leadership (e.g., a blue ribbon award). Purple is the color of royalty (as in the expression "born to the color of purple). Green is the color of the environment and health (e.g., Greenpeace, Healthy Choice).

Color can actually evoke physiological responses. For example, red has been shown to increase blood pressure rate, while cool blues and greens have been shown to decrease blood pressure rate.

Color has incredible psychological power and can provoke different sensory perceptions. McDonald's, for example, uses orange to stimulate customer appetites. Red is an in-your-face color that appears to move toward your eyes. Blue appears to move away from you.

When choosing a color for a brand or a logo, do not simply choose your favorite color. Use color to support your brand's message and personality. You may want to first focus on the mood you want to evoke, but other factors might override a choice based only on mood or tone. (For example, do not do it if it means copying your top competitor's color.)

BRAND TYPEFACES

Typography, like color, conveys personality and brand tone. For some brands, the typographical look can be so distinctive that it conveys the brand's essence in a single second (e.g., Toys 'R Us). Over time your typography becomes an extension of the language you use. Your words read differently in different typefaces.

SnowBoard   **Pain**

Thank You   **Gothic**

Logotypes send messages, too. A logotype does not equal the brand in the consumer's mind, but it does grab the consumer's attention, announce your name and give consumers a visual hook to hang your brand on. A logotype will not close sales, but a tacky one can certainly close doors. A bad logotype — a bad first impression — can encourage prospects to ignore you, or even convince them that you are not someone they want to do business with. A professional logo is part of looking professional. A bad logo — a bad first impression — can be enough to convince prospects to ignore you, that you are not someone they want to do business with.

When commissioning a logo, be sure to convey your brand essence to your graphic designer. The graphic interpretation should support your message of who you are, your image and your brand positioning. Ideally, your typography should symbolize the most important characteristic of your brand.

When choosing typefaces, consider legibility, uniqueness, and range of weights and widths (e.g., condensed or expanded). It is important to be distinctive, but it is also important to be *legible*.

Intelligent, intuitive typography...

- Supports your information hierarchy
- Conveys emotions
- Reflects positioning
- Works in a range of sizes
- Works in both color and black and white
- Differs from the competition's typography
- Reflects both your brand culture and your target market's culture
- Is compatible with your brand personality
- Is compatible with the brand mark

THE PACKAGE IT COMES IN

Packaging is a brand strategy disguised as a container. Until you package the product, it is just an idea.

Brand packaging matters. In addition to stimulating the senses, packaging creates an overall brand impression and offers hints about what you can expect from the brand. Packaging is often the first glimpse of a brand, and it can either repel or attract the consumer.

Because it is always a brand impression, packaging must be memorable. For example:

Tiffany's: Robin's-egg blue with black type

Macy's: Red star

Target: Red bulls-eye

Coke: Red, with white ribbon

Pepsi: Blue background with red, white and blue circle

SimpleHuman: bold colors with icon coding

Apple: Apple silhouette with a bite eaten

IBM: Blue (or white) I.B.M. letters dissected by lines

AT&T: White and blue striped globe

In retail especially, redesigned packaging can revive an outdated presentation for relatively little expense. A new container shape, larger brand iconography — even a clearer, easier-to-read label can push more products off the shelf. New packaging re-announces the brand and can suggest that the product is improved in some significant way.

Let us take a look at some examples…

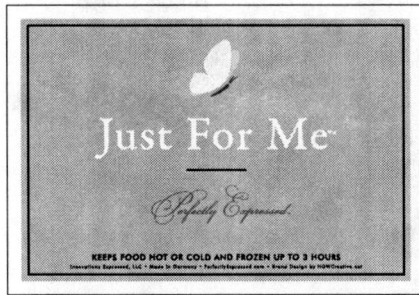

Perfectly Expressed™ creates hot- and cold-food picnic bags for homebound patients, packaged in an advanced polymer bag that allows meals to stay hot for three hours. The simple-yet-sophisticated muted-color motifs offered a homey grace note — elegance on the road.

Domino Sugar's new 4-pound canister is a great example of an innovative packaging revamp. The company wanted to create a more user-friendly package and boost flat sales, so they replaced the ubiquitous and unfriendly paper packaging. The easy-to-store plastic canister also enables the company to charge a premium for a package that actually contains less sugar. The canister has become one of Domino's best-selling retail items.

In 2002, Heinz wanted to increase functionality, so they designed an inverted, upside-down bottle. They revolutionized a 170-year-old industry and solved the customer's biggest complaint: It is hard to squeeze out that last bit of ketchup. The vacuum cap prevents that funky crust from forming around the lid. A year after the bottle's debut, Heinz ketchup sales rose 6 percent, while the overall ketchup industry increased only 2 percent. A Heinz official has been quoted as saying: "Companies make a lot of money by making things less annoying,"

Kraft redesigned its Chewy Chips Ahoy bag after discovering that customers often transferred Chips Ahoy cookies to jars for easy access and to avoid staleness. The new patented resealable opening on the top of the bag solved both problems, and nearly doubled sales over the old packaging.

When revamping packaging, there is one caveat: be sure to retain enough of the original look and feel so that you do not confuse customers and erode brand recognition and awareness. It will not do you any good to have a great new package if your customers do not recognize you.

INTUITIVE WEB DESIGN

Your website is a critical touchpoint. It is a 24/7 location — always open for business — that customers can visit again and again. They can visit on their lunch hour. They can visit in their pajamas in the wee hours of the morning. The website is still working even when you are not.

But a website is not a place the way McDonald's is a place. The website is just one step in the process of connecting to the customer, though it is an important step, especially in today's wired society. If someone wants to do a little quick research on your company, there's about a 90 percent chance that they'll hit the Web first. Your website will be the first impression for many of your potential customers.

How many websites have you visited recently that inspired you to buy on the spot? Odds are good that you can count them on one hand. These days, we are all digitally sophisticated, and we have come to rely on websites as a key touchpoint. For some e-commerce businesses, the website may be the *only* touchpoint. E-tailers live and die by the customer's website experience. For these companies, the website experience *is* the brand experience.

Despite these facts, most website designs, ironically, ignore the fundamentals, which are actually *essentials.* Ignoring the fundamentals will almost certainly guarantee that a site does not live up to customer expectations, which means it will never achieve the brand goals.

There is an order and hierarchy to page composition that applies not only to web sites, but to all other graphical touchpoints as well; e.g., ad layouts, posters, and packaging. Every design element must either be: *dominant, subdominant, or subordinant.* Otherwise, everything is shouting at the viewer at once. The result is that the mind can not absorb and process the information in a meaningful way, and it becomes difficult to compel the viewer to take action. Your call to action will drown in a muddy sea of debris.

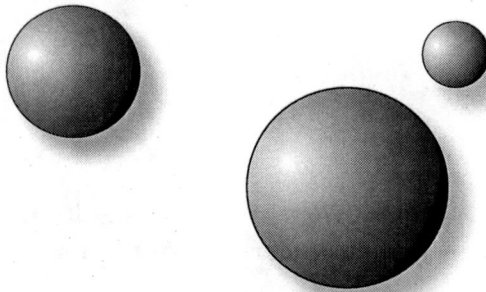

Great websites are a balance of aesthetics and functionality, practicality and creativity. You achieve that goal through these elements:

Visual Aesthetics: The coordination of visual elements to attract attention, win acceptance and produce impact.

Contrast: The benefits and values must LEAP OUT AND GRAB. Too often they do not.

Legibility: The message cannot get lost in the design, and neither can it get lost in the fog of its own rhetoric.

Reading Sequence: In a universe where one stumble will click buyers away, far too many sites are designed to drive readers to the exits.

Benefits not clearly defined: Low overhead? Tell them about it and do it quickly. Your website must grab the visitor's attention in 3 seconds or less or you are at risk of loosing them.

Develop your copy with these elements in mind...

The 3 Cs of Copywriting:

Contrast: Benefits must be communicated, and well. The value of your product or service must be emphasized. Benefits can not be alluded to, or hinted at, or left to conjecture. They have got to jump off the page! (Tastefully, of course.)

Clarity: If you are driving along and suddenly hit a patch of fog, you slow down. That is exactly what your prospects do when they hit a patch of foggy copy. Speak plainly, stay on point and make sure your message is clear. Say what needs to be said and nothing more. They're looking for an excuse to click off. Don't give it to them!

Continuum: Go with a sensible flow. Pull your prospect from sentence to sentence, paragraph to paragraph with tight, fluid copy. Imagine copy as a continuous thread being pulled tighter and tighter as it nears the end. If your prospect stumbles, or has to do a say-wha?, they will get annoyed click-off will quickly follow.

Create a compelling content structure:

1. Grab attention

2. Show relevance

3. Get to the benefits quickly

4. Make it easy for the customer to decide (and buy!)

> **STRATEGY SESSION:**

Think you have chosen the right graphic design assets? Take this litmus test for each element — brand icon, name, tagline, color(s), typeface...

1. Is the element distinctive — does it differentiate you from the competition?

2. Is the element aligned with your brand strategy?

3. Can the element be legally protected as part of your mark?

4. Will your element be flexible for a full range of applications and mediums beyond print; including for example, outdoor and broadcast advertising, kiosks, apparel?

(9)

Authentic Execution & the Business of Brand

An authentic brand strategy without thoughtful, purposeful execution is worthless. Without good execution, a plan is just a plan — a monument to what might have been. Brand execution is where you move the ball from the 20-yard line to the end zone. You can not score, after all, from the 20-yard line.

Doing it right means developing a detailed master execution plan that dovetails with your company's core business objectives. Doing it right can shave years of frustration off the brand-building curve and save a company the millions of dollars it might have otherwise spent on "experiments" that missed the mark.

When organizations are not clear about who they are and what they stand for — from the inside out — they have a tendency to devise touchpoints that look good on paper, but do not work in reality. It is easy to get sucked into an expensive start-stop, start-stop cycle of experiments that dilute the brand. The brand begins to falter. More expensive experiments ensue. The brand still fails to achieve a return on those investments.

Brand authenticity is more than a strategy. Your execution must be authentic, too.

EXTENDING THE BRAND IDENTITY ACROSS ALL TOUCHPOINTS

Touchpoints are contact points, lead generators, greeters, and the primary drivers of brand equity and brand value. Thousands of companies fail because they could not communicate the complete brand experience through an integrated set of touchpoints: One voice, one message — a unified, authentic story.

To accomplish this, you must map every step of the customer's journey — from awareness to experience and finally, loyalty. Every brand is built on experiences. And each touchpoint is a new opportunity to differentiate the brand from its competition and reinforce customer loyalty.

Customers determine the meaning and the value of a brand over time; in other words, brand-building is a process, and it happens over time. One touchpoint encounter might make a great first impression, but if subsequent touchpoint encounters do not hold up their end of the bargain, you can lose a customer you had, or turn a prospect who was on the verge of becoming a customer into a prospect who flips to your competitor's brand.

Authentic touchpoints are valuable brand assets. But faulty touchpoints can turn valuable brand assets into liabilities.

What touchpoints are needed to build trust and loyalty? Here are some elements to consider:

- Sales promotions
- Advertising
- Publications
- Newsletter
- Business forms
- Signage
- Packaging
- Exhibits
- Proposals
- Emails
- Voice mails

- Websites
- Web banners
- Letterheads
- Business cards
- Publicity
- Services
- Products
- Employees
- Speeches
- Presentations
- Networking
- Telephone
- Word of mouth
- Trade shows
- Direct mail
- Public relationships
- Public affairs
- Affinity marketing
- Viral marketing
- Cell phone voicemail greetings

PLANNING THE EXECUTION

1. Define your brand-building goals. Let's say your sales were 50 million last year and you want to do 100 million this year. Outline strategies that have the potential to double your sales.

   A. Define your short-term (3-month) objectives/goals, and outline

the action you would take to accomplish each.

B. Define your long-term objectives/goals, and outline the action you would take to accomplish each.

2. Outline your Touchpoint Plan with completion dates.

A simple chart like this will help you get organized…

Month 1

A. Touchpoint:

B. Time-Frame:

C. Investment:

D. Measurable Results:

Use this process guide to draft your touchpoint plan…

Application brand design essentials

1. Convey the brand personality

2. Align with positioning strategy

3. Create a point of view and a look and feel

4. Make it work across all media

5. Demonstrate understanding of the target customer

6. Differentiate

Packaging process

1. Identify all goals and objectives for the package

2. Research competitive product packaging

3. Identify functional criteria and align with product/brand

4. Positioning

5. Identify any relevant legal requirements

6. Design and develop the prototype

7. Determine production specs and costs

8. Identify design and production experts and providers

9. Produce packaging

Website process

1. Draft website blueprint

2. Define layout and navigational structure

3. Identify technical/software engineering needs; develop specs

4. Develop content and graphic design prototype

5. Develop technical/programming concept

6. Launch site and maintain

Signage design process

1. Identify all goals and objectives for the signage

2. Research competitor signage

3. Identify design team

4. Identify all media, formats and usage; e.g., outdoor, vehicle, kiosk, trade shows, etc.

5. Identify functional criteria and align with product/brand positioning

6. Develop and document schematics and production specs for each medium

7. Develop copy and graphic design prototypes

8. Identify production experts and fabrication providers

9. Fabricate and maintain

Other touchpoints to consider:

Services, Products, Employees, Speeches, Presentation, General Media, Signage, Events, Posters, Book, DVD's, Packaging, Networking, Telephone, Word of mouth, Publicity, Website, Business cards, Ads, Direct mail, Civic Marketing, Sales promotion, Advertising, Newsletter, Business forms, Exhibits Proposals, E-Mails, Voice mails, Web banners, Publicity, Greeters, To-go menus, TV, Trade shows, Invitation – Personal, Apparel, Magazines.

THE COMPLETE BRAND CAMPAIGN: INTEGRATING YOUR TOUCHPOINTS

When executing a complete brand campaign, all your touchpoints must be integrated to tell a consistent, authentic story. The following case studies will take you behind the scenes of three complete brand campaign executions…

CASE STUDY: Piano Wizard

Background. Piano Wizard® combines the fun of a video game with the fundamentals of playing a piano. With Piano Wizard, a child is playing the piano almost from the instant the game is started. They learn intuitively to hit the right note at the right time. Gradually, as their skill level advances, so does the game's challenge level. Before one knows it, the child has learned to read music.

Challenge. A small team consisting of key client and HOW Creative personnel met to bring the Piano Wizard idea into reality. Together, they designed the Graphic User Interface, the character design, the tradeshow booth, advertising, merchandise, plus all branding — brand identity, brand architecture, brand positioning and brand value, while also identifying the target audiences within various industries.

Positioning. We positioned the product as an education and entertainment platform—non-violent and of appeal to the entire family. Distribution was through retailers Apple, Target and Radio Shack, plus via the Internet and educational programs.

Results. Introduced in 2005, the Piano Wizard immediately received rave reviews in Wired Magazine, Wallstreet Journal, Fox News, ABC, NBC, CBS News. It also won multiple awards such as Top Toy of the Year Award, Nappa Gold, The Toy Man – Seal of Approval, iParenting Media Winner Awards, eChoice Award and Computer Times Editor's choice. These honors lead to licensing agreements with Fisher Price, Hanna Montana, Billy Joel, and many more. All this gave rise to building brand value and brand equity in the millions.

CASE STUDY: City of Los Angeles Marathon

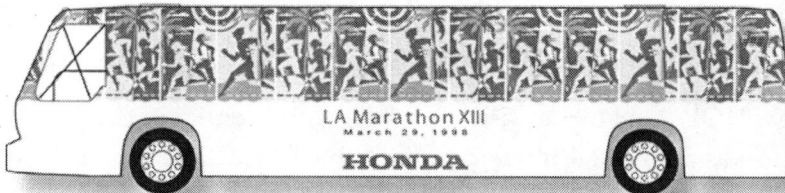

LA Marathon XIII
March 29, 1998

HONDA

BEFORE

AFTER

Background. The City of Los Angeles Marathon, sponsored by Honda, is the largest event marathons in the world, and ranks among the premiere marathons in the U.S. Fitting of an entertainment capital, the LA event features more live entertainment per mile than any other race in the world (85 performing groups), and draws an audience of more than one million spectators. As an additional duty, HOW Creative was assigned to re-brand the City of Los Angeles Bike Tour, sponsored by Aura. This event was linked to the marathon events in all communications efforts.

Challenge. In previous years, the event had failed to establish a unique brand identity. HOW Creative wanted to give it that identity, while promoting the marathon with new energy and life. Standing as a possible hindrance to this goal: the client had a smaller media budget to work with than in the previous year.

Strategy. HOW Creative envisioned the brand identity of the LA Marathon as a simple, bold and memorable visual. The use of form, function, structure and color across all applications was deemed vital to the success of the brand identity campaign.

It was determined to use yellow as the primary color against the complimentary color of a blue sky. The typography for event dates was increased to be easily read at a distance. Stylized illustrator runners captured the high-energy of the event, while adding a laid-back tone. The dynamism and simplicity of the design, as used on vehicle wraps, was readily perceptible within just 1.3 seconds. This design successfully increased brand awareness and proved to be the key to radically attracting new runners, attendees, and event vendors.

Execution. With more than 25 Authentic Touch Points (applications) of the brand icon and brand design, the greatest challenge was in creating an integrated campaign. HOW Creative managed to do this by keeping the concept simple, bold and memorable.

From entertainment venues for the more than 85 performing groups along the route, the City of Los Angeles Marathon proved to be a city-wide celebration. HOW Creative positioned and re-branded the entire campaign from city bus signs to street banners to the actual medal awards.

The event drew a record-breaking, sold-out event with 23,000 participants—the largest event in the 15-year history of the marathon.

Results. We reignited the torch of the City of Los Angeles Marathon with a simple, bold and memorable brand identity system. HOW Creative's brand graphics drew a record breaking, sold out event with 23,000 participants—the largest event in the 15-year history of the marathon. It resulted in increased business revenues, tighter community bonds, and increases in brand value and equity.

CASE STUDY: Stander

BEFORE

AFTER

Background. Stander Inc. is unique in the totality of its approach to product development—broadly invested in the invention, manufacture and distribution of innovative mobility solutions for the bed, couch, car and bathroom. Founded by Jan Miller in 1998, Stander's primary focus is the durable medical equipment cash-and- carry market. All Stander products retail for under $199.

Standers' primary focus is product development. In pursuit of that goal, they are dedicated to recruiting the industry's best and brightest engineers and patent attorneys, and pledged to bringing 2-4 new products to market each year, Stander has developed a reputation for developing products that are unique to the market. In product categories where Stander faces competition, they are the low-price leader by a wide margin.

Stander maintains its price leadership position by value-engineering products to keep quality high and prices low.

Challenge. Having secured a strong niche in the durable medical equipment industry, Stander expanded its vision to the mass retail market. In this new business model, they quickly learned that many of the lessons they had learned in achieving their leadership position had to be rethought—and revamped.

Positioning. The company realized that, while its products were ready for mass retail distribution, its brand image would likely hold it back from taking that giant step. It was at this time they attended a HOW Creative Strategic DNA session, where they learned lessons that introduced them to a business strategy linked to a brand strategy. After three intense days, they left with a redefined and much more solid business model for creating multiple revenue streams. Here, they also developed their:

- Brand Vision
- Brand Philosophy
- Consumer aspiration
- Brand Promise
- Emotional drivers
- Brand position
- Core message
- New brand name
- Primary brand colors
- Slogan

These all lead to a concrete plan and timeline for reinventing their brand identity and entering the mass retail market.

Results. The client in this communication best summarized the positive outcomes of all branding efforts:

"In the 7 months following our brand strategy meeting, sales grew by 32%. No new products were brought to market during those 7 months. Thanks in large part to our new brand identity, we successfully landed and grew accounts with the following mass retailers:

1. Walmart

2. Costco

3. Target

4. Sears

5. K-Mart

6. Walgreens

7. CVS

8. Rite Aid

9. Amazon

10. Overstock

11. Drugstore.com

INTERNAL BRANDING: INTERNAL TOUCHPOINTS COUNT, TOO

One of the biggest mistakes a company can make is failing to embrace an inside-out approach to brand-building. Many companies are too focused on the product brand strategy, not realizing that part of the secret to authenticity is building a strong internal brand culture.

Authentic brands are inside-out brands: The corporate culture aligns with the brand identity and projects out into the world. Authenticity is about more than a snazzy icon, catchy taglines and expensive ad campaigns — the external stuff. It is an embedded cultural approach to branding that guides communications to all stakeholders — from customer promotional materials to personnel policies, management development programs, and fund-raising and other socially responsible initiatives. In the new economy, sustainability requires companies to become more accountable to all constituencies, which includes, for starters, both employees and customers.

It is true that outside-in approaches can create high visibility and some tangible sizzle, but they tend to produce only short-term results. The sizzle can fizzle once the applause subsides.

Inside-out branding helps organizations overcome internal resistance to branding efforts and extend the brand beyond traditional measures to true innovation and authenticity. When marketers develop brand strategies that are not supported across all the internal touchpoints (e.g., customer service reps), employees end up feeling betrayed and frustrated, as do customers. Ultimately, the brand reputation suffers, and the branding initiative becomes a scapegoat for the company's larger problems; for example, if brand value takes a dive and long-term equity is eroding faster than a Malibu mudslide.

Sometimes brand executers feel pressured to execute a brand strategy in a short time-frame. They are marching to the ticking of a clock, knocking off those external touchpoints, one by one — the mark, the ads, the taglines — completely ignoring the crucial internal branding process. Marketers have been trained, after all, to focus on *external* targets — customers. And often, they do not take time to engage employees in the brand-building process.

Sometimes it is just a simple matter of communication. Many companies have a "departmental mentality" — a silo culture — instead of a holistic, whole-brain culture. Most employees assume they will be excluded from the branding process and do not try to engage.

This problem is so easy to fix! Establish an internal communication system that fosters meaningful dialogue about the brand identity. The core essence of every brand depends on how well the company clarifies the behavior it needs from employees in order to deliver on the brand promise. In addition to how well the company builds a culture of *involvement*. When employees are engaged in the brand-building process and believe that the company values their input, they take ownership and the brand gains valuable brand champions.

One of your most valuable tangible assets will be brand-passionate employees, authentic storytellers who spread your message and personify your values, and help you cultivate brand equity. Starbucks, for example, is often cited as a successful inside-out brand culture. At the Starbucks stores, you can actually see the employee buy-in, positive customer-employee dialogue, and on-brand behavior. In other words, you see the brand personality and style reflected in the employees.

The more internal brand champions you have, the stronger your brand will be.

Successful internal branding starts with the involvement of the CEO and senior management and trickles down. Brand champions help make the brand relevant for their colleagues. They do not have to be senior managers. They do not have to be experts on branding. Their most important qualification is *enthusiasm.*

The idea of brand begins to resonate with employees when it begins to affect the way they do their everyday work. They must be inspired by the brand and see the benefit of engaging with it. Brand champions deliver on the brand promise on a day-to-day basis. Brand champions transform the brand into something that has meaning for the whole company…and ultimately for the customer.

Every customer brand experience has a defining moment that will determine how a customer responds. Mapping a complete customer brand experience will help you identify every possible opportunity for a human-to-human customer connection.

Faulty internal branding results in weak connections, and conflicting brand messages are almost guaranteed. An authentic brand is a consistent brand.

SHORTENING THE SELL-THROUGH TRAJECTORY

Authentic touchpoints shorten the sell-through trajectory. The faster you become believable and trustable, the shorter the path to the close.

In the new economy, we forge relationships with strategic partners whose goals align with our goals, and whose market or customer base intersects with ours. We forge strategic alliances in innovative new ways, often deploying technology to accelerate growth and revenue; for example, plugging into a strategic partner's existing customer database. It is a whole lot faster than building your own database.

You can shave years off the brand-building curve, and literally catapult a brand into the marketplace overnight. Take it from FedEx, who knows a thing or two about overnight delivery. When Kinko's and FedEx joined forces to put FedEx stations in Kinko's locations (now called FedEx Office), FedEx exponentially multiplied market share and penetration — once again, overnight.

Look for shortcuts in your selling cycle to generate profits quicker. And by "shortcuts," we mean doing things *smarter*, not shabbier.

Start by analyzing customer flow-through. Diagram your sales flow-through, step by step, from your lead generators to the close. Do you see steps that could be eliminated? Or steps whose lead-time could be shortened? For example, one solution is to create an educational website that leads the customer through your entire sales process. Providing substantive online educational tools empowers customers and helps them reach decisions faster and without the usual overhead.

CASE VIGNETTE

A noted cosmetic surgeon who specializes in reconstructive cosmetic surgery developed a comprehensive website that not only increased national awareness of his brand, but allowed both current and potential customers to explore in-depth information about the benefits of his innovative cosmetic procedures. The site educated prospects and effectively presold his services, allowing him to eliminate time-consuming prescreening calls and shave considerable time off the sell-through cycle, time which could be applied to billable patient care. He quickly doubled his gross income.

MAXIMIZING YOUR BRAND ECOSYSTEM

Every brand's ecosystem can be expanded — *always*. There are always undiscovered new species of customer and untapped new species of strategic partner out there, just waiting for you to discover them.

Following are some tactics for discovery...

EXPAND YOUR BRAND MARKET SPACE

What partners might be attracted to your Authentic Brand Ecosystem? Look for ways to define your market space and create uncontested mindshare. Investigate other channels and industries. Talk to your resellers and buyers. Scan the brandscape for potential partners who offer complementary products and services.

Seek out strategic partners who share your brand culture, core philosophy, values and vision — compatibility in business marriages (as in all marriages) is essential. By all accounts, the Fed-Ex-Kinko's marriage has been a happy one. AOL-Time Warner's troubled marriage, on the other hand, has been widely chronicled in the media; their two cultures did not mesh.

And scan the future horizon. Pay special attention to hot trends and topics in the public's collective consciousness that you can piggyback, including short-term trends that you can react to quickly, and trends that you believe have staying power and will drive market direction. Notice how trends differ among generations. How can you make your business model more flexible? Look for ways that technology can help you innovate.

EXPAND YOUR CUSTOMER CORE

Thorough, accurate customer profiling will help you uncover innovative new ways to expand your core customer base and reach beyond existing demand.

Use the customer profile tactics you learned in Chapter 3 to pinpoint prospects who:

1. No longer purchase your products and/or service?

2. No longer purchase your products and/or service in your existing category?

3. Are now purchase your products and/or service alternative products?

4. May not understand the aspiration and value of your product and/or category. How can you educate them on it?

Identify features and benefits these market segments seek that are not currently being met. How can you reach these prospects? Build on common aspirations that extend to people who are not currently customers, rather than focusing on existing customers. If your complete brand identity is broadcast consistently through your touchpoints, you'll nab new species of customers who relate to your core values.

Is your brand image conveying your true brand identity? Many companies are not aware that the perception they are creating in the eyes of customers does not align with their brand positioning and brand values. Often, it is the simplest details that confuse or repel customers, and become an obstacle to closing the sale. If your brochure is vague, if your website is cold and formal and does not communicate who you really are and why a prospect should choose your brand, you've created an obstacle.

If you are looking for a particular top-quality product and you walk into a shop that has a cement garage floor and an ancient metal 1970s desk, chances are, you will be tempted to walk away. That shabby storefront is a touchpoint that doesn't communicate the level of quality you are seeking.

Scrutinize all your touchpoints. Eliminate any obstacle that's costing you business.

WHAT ARE YOUR SALES GOALS?

What were your sales last year? What were your sales projections for this year? You might use a quick spreadsheet like this.

Last Year: Total Sales: _____

Services: $_____=____% of total sales

Units: $_____=____% of total sales

Sales team: $_____=____% of total sales

Affiliates: $_____=____% of total sales

Strategic Partners: $_____=____% of total sales

This Year: Total Sales Projection: _____

Services: $_____=____% of total sales

Units: $_____=____% of total sales

Sales team: $_____=____% of total sales

Affiliates: $_____=____% of total sales

Strategic Partners: $_____=____% of total sales

Now that you have created a living, breathing brand and can see what is possible for its future, how would you re-forecast your sales revenue for this year?

Take a look at your financial assets. Now take that list of assets, and remember, that it is bigger than the warehouses and office buildings your company owns. It includes your brand assets — the tangible, visual assets plus the intangibles

Look for liabilities. Got faulty touchpoints? Customer service reps who do not support the brand tone and personality? Fix them or fire them. Is your brand message and personality consistent across all your promotional materials in both graphic design and copy? Fix it.

Your brand should be a lighthouse that projects far and wide into the fog of traditional corporate financial assets and liabilities.

⑩

Managing the Brand For Equity & Value

Aggressive brand management matters. Maintaining brand authenticity and keeping a brand viable in the modern marketplace requires skill, savvy, innovation and unfailing devotion to detail.

Remember: Brands are a shortcut to a Buy decision. It takes less energy, time and money to keep an existing customer than to get a new one — one more reason to make sure you deliver on your brand promise, again and again.

The brand management mantra is this: Every move you make should advance the brand's equity and value. Continue to advance your brand — day by day, week by week, year by year.

AUDITING YOUR BRAND

Hire a policeman (policeperson). Every brand needs a brand manager who will police the brand on an ongoing to ensure that the brand stays true to its core values and always, unswervingly delivers on its promise.

Most brand managers tend to focus too heavily on the rational, business aspects of the brand. And sure, somebody's got to stay on top of that stuff, too. But a left-brain brand manager must be surrounded with right-brainers who remain true to the brand's creative and aesthetic vision, and never lose sight of the fact that a brand, in the end, must engage the consumer and stimulate an emotional response.

Your best bet is to hire the best whole-brain thinker you can find. And hold regular Brand Ideas Meetings every few weeks. Pick a date. And stick to it. Bad things happen to brands when their owners run out of ideas.

Review each of your touchpoints. Streamline your infrastructure so that your delivery becomes automatic. You can always find a new idea to explore, and a new way to boost your emotional bond with customers. You can always find a new way to engage new internal brand champions. Sometimes the best new ideas can come from quiet corners.

Discuss lots of ideas and view them from every possible angle. For fresh perspectives, use different media to present the same idea; for example, both large-screen video and physical 3-D models. Repurpose old ideas…seek out innovative, emotion-provocative ways to make old ideas new, while retaining your core brand identity. That's how you perpetuate emotional bonds with customers and continue to stay relevant in the marketplace.

If your brand does not accomplish all the following, rebrand. Otherwise, your brand will fade away.

Brand Audit Checklist:

- Does your brand convey instantly your unique purchase proposition?
- Is your unique purchase proposition viable and thrivable in the current market climate?
- How deep and how broad is your brand awareness? Does your brand inspire instant recall and recognition in the customer's mind?
- Are all your touchpoints integrated? Compelling? Authentic?
- Have you identified the market obstacles that are impeding your growth. Have you got an action plan to remove those obstacles?
- Is your brand returning a satisfactory profit?
- Does it continue to build value and equity?

STICK TO THE RULES: BRAND GUIDELINES

Would Barbie still seem like Barbie if someone decided that Barbie pink should be brown? Make Coke blue, and it turns it into Pepsi. Make UPS purple and orange and it turns into FedEx.

You can not always count on your strategic partners, franchisees or licensees to properly represent your brand. Make it easy for them to do it right. Develop a Brand Guidelines manual (sometimes referred to as a Brand Style Guide) to limit your exposure and enforce it. Consistency, consistency, consistency — across all touchpoints, all partnerships; this is how you maintain control of your brand identity for growth and expansion.

Faulty touchpoints dilute, distort, and damage your brand. It happens easier than you think...

Imagine that a licensee or co-op marketer decides to stretch or squish your brand icon to better fit the space in a magazine ad... Or uses some dreadfully amateurish typeface for your brand name (picture the Nike swoosh with *Nike* typeset in Old English!). They have just cheapened you, bastardized your brand identity, and misrepresented who you are. And they have compromised one of your visual (and financial!) assets.

In addition to graphical brand design standards (Dos and Don'ts), your Brand Guidelines manual should detail your company mission, core brand values and message. It should be educational, user-friendly, efficient, and readily accessible to both internal and external stakeholders.

Make Guidelines freely available to all your partners, and keep it updated. The Internet makes it a snap to consolidate brand management communications in one place, and in an inexpensive and easy-to-update format. Consider developing a stakeholders extranet. Provide employees, vendors and affiliates with user-friendly access to brand resources. Provide them with downloadable materials — logo and ad slicks, style templates.

In addition to a Brand Guidelines manual, your package could include:

- Marketing and Sales Toolkits, for companies with independent distributors

- Thought Books that communicate the central unifying principles of your touchpoints plan

- Identity Standards CD. Could provide PDF versions of your Brand Guidelines and everything from white papers and marketing tools to design layouts for trade show booths. You could also provide dazzling colorful animations that demonstrate your brand value and illustrate your brand message.

DAZZLE YOUR STAKEHOLDERS: PRESENTATIONS TO INVESTORS AND BUYERS

Every presentation you do — whether it's directed to investors or buyers — should aim for the mind, heart and gut.

How do you engage stakeholders? First, present polished ideas. Do not leave anything to the viewer's imagination. Stakeholders want to be persuaded. They want to be entertained. That means you must go beyond The Powerpoint Presentation to a Whole-Brained Presentation. A dispassionate handful of bullet-point slides aim for the intellect, not the heart and gut.

In the old economy, we presented the sketchy mockups — marketing renderings — and hoped our audiences would fill in the visual blanks. In the new economy, we can do better — much better. We can inexpensively create gorgeous four-color presentation boards and 3-D models. Visual aids *illustrate* your brand's value.

But pretty is not enough, especially if you are presenting to investors. Accompany the pretty stuff with a strong business overview that presents the logical, practical, rational (functional) aspects of your business model. Talk about profit margins, how you plan to make money. Demonstrate your brand's inherent value and equity, and why the brand is sustainable. Talk about your core competencies and your internal branding — demonstrate value on the inside. Discuss liabilities openly and honestly, then show why liability is limited. Focus on showing what is *possible* — from co-branding opportunities to future line extensions.

When you are presenting to partners who will help you sell product, show how the functional and emotional benefits must be crafted to assure purchase action from customers. Show how your brand fulfills aspirations and how it will make an emotional connection. When it comes to the customer, remember: Emotional always trumps rational.

PREDICTING THE FUTURE: IT'S ABOUT THE CATEGORY

To build a new brand, you must overcome the logical notion of *serving* a market. Focus on *creating* a market. New branding opportunities almost always lie in creating new markets, not pursuing existing markets.

Take Coca-Cola. How did they become a megabrand? In those days (100-something years ago), the soft-drink market consisted of such beverages as lemonade, root beer, sarsparilla, ginger ale, orange and grape drinks. Coke became a big brand because it created a new market called *cola*. Coca-Cola did not just create a new product. They created a whole new *category*.

What you are about to read may shock you, but here goes: Market size is irrelevant. That's right — irrelevant. What was the size of the cola market when Coca-Cola was launched? Zero. What was the size of the fast food hamburger market when McDonald's opened their first store? Zero.

> Sometimes, customers do not know they want something until you give it to them.

> Create a new category that you can be first in. Then create a brand so authentic that you can imprint your brand on that category.

> • Saran Wrap was the first plastic food wrap.

> • Q-tips was the first cotton swab.

> • Pampers was the first disposable baby diaper.

> • Kleenex was the first pocket tissue.

> • Get the idea?

THE SECRET TO WINNING BRAND BATTLES

How can you compete against a household-name brand like Kleenex or Q-Tip that has become a generic? You can not. It is next to impossible to overtake a generic. Why? Because you were not first. But that does not mean you cannot win the battle…

You compete with a generic by creating a new category. Narrow your focus. Think in sets and subsets and specializations. Fed-Ex, for example, commandeered a narrow segment of the courier category by creating a new subcategory: overnight delivery.

Do not try to compete against the #1 brand by doing what they do, hoping that you can capture a fraction of their market. Do *the opposite* of what they do. Uniqueness will beat trend-following every time.

Creating a powerful new brand means looking for ways to divide and conquer. How can your product or service can diverge from the existing category? Exploit divergence to create a new category that your brand can own. Over time, categories almost always diverge, with or without you. Knowing that divergence always happens helps you pinpoint the right time to act.

Now, once *you* become the leading brand, you can count on competitors popping up, and some of your customers will venture off to try the competitor's brand. It is usually better to let them go and focus your energy on attracting new customers. Grow the market, instead of trying to expand your brand to win the defectors back. That is how you maintain brand purity — authenticity. That is how you make sure you still stand for something in the customer's mind. The new brand that defines a category will almost always outsell the old brand that was stretched to encompass the new category.

If you are the minor player, you win the line-extension war by encouraging the new category to diverge. Create a new category, and put some distance between your new category and the old category. In doing so, you differentiate your new category (and your brand) from the dominant brand.

Consider the mass merchandiser battle of Wal-Mart vs. K-Mart vs. Target...

Wal-Mart was the original divergence story. They located stores only in small communities, while K-Mart — then the largest discount chain — built stores in larger cities. Then K-Mart and Target began to lose market share to brand behemoth Wal-Mart. K-Mart abandoned Blue Light Specials for Wal-Mart's "always low prices" pricing model (known in the industry as the Everyday Low Price or ELP model). Target, on the other hand, diverged to "mass with class." Classier displays, wide aisles, affordable designer merchandise. Target, effectively, created a whole new category: upscale mass merchandiser.

The bottom line? Wal-Mart is losing share, K-Mart filed bankruptcy and Target is ascendant.

Brands must be flexible enough to adapt to market and competitive changes. Think category first and brand second.

COMPETITION IS A GOOD THING

Competition, believe it or not, can actually be good for your brand. Competition tends to broaden a category, which increases the size of the market. The more companies there are out there promoting a category, the more convinced people become that they need that product category. From there, it is up to you differentiate your product and aim squarely and psychographically for your target. And one more thing: If your quality is better than the competition's, you have got a good shot at winning back the customers who defected, anyway.

The holy grail of brand leadership that you are searching for can only be attained by owning a category. If you are the leading brand; the best competitive strategy is to fight competing categories, not competing brands. Your goal is to *own a category*. The ultimate value of a brand is directly related to whether or not it stands for a category. Lowe's has encroached upon Home Depot's territory in recent years, and Home Depot no longer stands for the category "home improvement warehouse." Home Depot is struggling.

Brand strength depends on category strength. Long-term opportunities lie in categories, not brands. That is why it is important to promote the category. Do not just promote your brand. If people decide they no longer want high-end coffee, Starbucks brand loses much of its brand equity, and will have to dramatically diverge or die. But Starbucks, wisely, continues to promote the category — the high-end coffee *experience*.

But be prepared: Over time, some categories die. The brandscape is littered with dead categories. Does anyone still use freestanding Caller ID devices? In modern phones, Caller ID is built-in. If the category is dead, create a new one.

Thought is the catalyst of change. Launch a new brand with the goal of shaping behavior and introducing new thinking. The marketplace changes so rapidly that fresh insight is currency.

Be a thought leader. Contribute new thoughts to your industry. Infuse old processes with innovative ideas, and have the confidence to promote them. Thought leadership engages consumers and motivates them to listen to you.

Thought leadership is a vital driver of brand leadership, and ultimately, of business success. The brand that maintains thought leadership rules its market niche. In an information-driven economy, the thought leaders will be The Leaders.

How fast is a brand supposed to grow? Brand growth usually takes patience and steadfast dedication to purpose. Brands that take off at warp speed often burn out, lose relevance and turn out to be fads. (Seen any Bartles and Jaymes wine coolers lately?) Properly executed and managed, brands can evolve over time to become more dominant. Slow-growing hardwood trees outlive fast-growing softwood trees.

WHEN TO KILL THE BRAND AND WHEN TO REINVENT

You created a new category and you are the leading brand...

But that unique category of yours that grabbed so much attention is not so unique anymore. Sales have been steadily declining... every new promotional campaign seems to fall on deaf ears...

It is time to realistically assess your brand's value in the marketplace, diagnose its weaknesses, and decide whether to euthanize it or reinvent it. When a brand goes awry, it goes awry for a specific and consistent set of reasons — reasons that are identifiable, quantifiable and comprehensible. Sometimes what's called for is examining your brand under a microscope, rather than scanning the horizon with binoculars.

How do you know if it is time to put your brand out of its misery? These litmus tests will help you decide:

1. If the category is dead, pull the plug.

2. If the brand — and the ideas it stands for — is obsolete, pull the plug, even if the brand is "well-known." Well-known does not necessarily translate to continued profits and long-term equity.

3. If the brand has generated lackluster sales for years, is well-known, but has never really owned an idea in the public's mind, pull the plug. No brand lives forever. Instead of investing time and money in resuscitating an obsolete brand — an effort which will almost certainly fail — invest your resources in your next brand, your next category. Invest in the future.

That said, it is absolutely possible to save a brand that passes these litmus tests. There is a difference between an ailing brand and an obsolete brand. Losing the leadership position doesn't destroy a brand. In most markets, there is a lot of money to be made in the #2 and #3 slots. And the truth is, most customers have no idea who the #1 brand is. If they are loyal to your brand, they figure it is you. Do Pepsi-lovers know that Coke is the cola category leader? Do they care? If they knew, would they stop drinking Pepsi?

If you own an idea in the marketplace, and that idea isn't obsolete, reinvent and reinvigorate the brand. But if your decision is to reinvent, get on with it. Don't lose any more time. And do it with gusto, or don't bother. Minute tinkerings will not save an ailing brand.

Clever reinventions become brand advancements that continue to contribute to market dominance, year after year. The key to reinvention is capitalizing on your brand equity before it deteriorates in the marketplace. Do not wait until the brand is in trouble. Reinvent cyclically, like clockwork. It is one of the best strategies going for maintaining brand leadership.

Gillette, for example, reinvents shaving every few years. Two-bladed razors, adjustable two-bladed razors, shock-absorbent razors, three-bladed razors, "progressively aligned blades," "forward pivot action," male-only razors and female-only razors. Gillette has always got a new trick up their sleeve and a new category of shaving to create. It is true that they spend a fortune on R&D and patents. But the return on their investment is reflected in their continued category dominance and sustained brand equity.

BRAND CRISIS MANAGEMENT

Combatting negative publicity is perhaps the most difficult brand management task of all. There is no stronger test of a brand than a publicity crisis, and it can happen to the best of brands.

Negative publicity can destroy a brand and — thanks to the Internet and the proliferation of 24/7 cable news channels — literally overnight. Some of the most expensive and disastrous brand problems have occurred because something a company takes for granted suddenly stops working... a quality control process, a safety policy, a communication strategy. Once a crisis happens, there is no time for planning. That is why it is important to have a crisis management plan in place *before* a crisis occurs.

E. coli and Salmonella have a lot to teach us about brand crisis management. These two malicious bacteria have ravaged major food brands in recent years. Nothing, it seems, is safe from them — beef, pistachio nuts, spinach, strawberries, peanut butter products. Yes, microscopic bacteria has dinged the reputations of such stellar household names as Kellogg, Keebler, Peter Pan and Dole — not to mention the United States Food and Drug Administration (FDA).

Remember the infamous 2008 Salmonella contamination case of peanut paste supplier, Peanut Corp. of America? For over a year, this company knowingly continued to ship Salmonella-tainted peanut butter products that. By early 2009, they were fleeing the brandscape through bankruptcy protection and trying to figure out how to escape federal criminal charges.

If a near-invisible microorganism can destroy decades-old brand equity, all brands are at risk. But when crisis strikes, the difference between a sustainable brand and a dead brand is good brand management. It's all about how you handle the crisis.

Johnson & Johnson's handling of the "Tylenol Tampering Crisis" stands in stark contrast to Peanut Corp. of America. In 1982, cyanide was discovered in Tylenol capsules, a product used by an estimated 100 million people. The incident was a media debacle of potentially catastrophic proportions for manufacturer Johnson & Johnson. But Johnson & Johnson took a proactive approach. They cooperated fully with the government and the media from the outset, announcing an immediate recall of all Tylenol packages. They accepted responsibility, told the truth, and maintained an open line of communication with the public.

Johnson & Johnson had a socially responsible plan in place *before* the crisis struck. They were prepared for both crisis communication and crisis management. And despite the saturated media coverage, they managed to dilute the negative publicity.

The result? Johnson & Johnson earned high praise from the media and high integrity marks from the public. They quickly introduced innovative tamper-resistant packaging, generating even more positive follow-up publicity. Despite the "tainted product," the brand's image — and long-term brand equity and value — was preserved.

The secret to brand crisis management is no different from the secret to successful brand-building: *Be Authentic.* Here are some strategies for managing negative publicity:

- **Don't be an ostrich.** Don't hide. Be visible and available for comment. Be proactive. Act quickly and decisively.

- **Express empathy sincerely and offer help immediately.** Never lose sight of the fact that you're communicating with other humans, who may be injured, confused, anxious or angry. Tell people how to get help and demonstrate your commitment to resolving the problem quickly and equitably. Update information frequently. Information reduces anxiety.

- **Tell the Truth.** Whatever you do, don't lie. If your company made a mistake, admit it up front. Lies and misinformation will only backfire. Remember, you are asking an untrusting public to trust you again.

- **Provide an ethical and socially responsible solution.** People will remember how you handled the incident, even those who are not personally impacted by it.

- **Use the 24/7 news machine to your advantage.** In the old economy, the first twenty-four hours was the critical response window. In the new economy, you are lucky if you have an hour. Remember that news outlets must fill the airwaves and column inches with something. Help them. Use this opportunity to control the message.

- **Move out of Crisis Mode quickly.** Resolve the crisis quickly and communicate how you resolved it. The longer you are perceived as being "in crisis," the more negative the media coverage becomes, the lower you drop in public opinion, and the deeper the damage to your brand's equity. Think long-term when you make decisions.

GO FORTH AND BE AUTHENTIC

What is an authentic brand? A brand so authentic that no competitor can duplicate it.

You'll find that the pursuit of authenticity is a rewarding journey. An authentic brand is a living, breathing thing. It is as human as the humans who created it, and watch over it every single day.

CPSIA information can be obtained at www.ICGtesting.com
Printed in the USA
239645LV00004B/55/P